BroadStreet Publishing Group, LLC.
Savage, Minnesota, USA
Broadstreetpublishing.com

365 Days of Courage

© 2023 by BroadStreet Publishing®

9781424565733
9781424565740 (eBook)

Devotional entries composed by Sara Perry.

Typesetting and design by Garborg Design Works | garborgdesign.com

Editorial services by Michelle Winger | literallyprecise.com and Carole Holdahl.

Printed in China.

23   24   25   26   27   28   7   6   5   4   3   2   1

"This is my command—
be strong and courageous!
Do not be afraid or discouraged.
For the LORD your God is with you
wherever you go."

JOSHUA 1:9 NLT

Introduction

Courage isn't something that comes naturally to most. The only way to truly be brave is to walk in the confidence that comes from knowing God, relying on him to be your strength. When you spend time with him, he will fill you with peace and hope for the future. When you finally see yourself as God sees you, you will recognize the talents and abilities you have been blessed with and start operating in the fullness of those gifts.

Be encouraged with truth as you spend time with God, reflecting on these devotions, Scriptures, and prayers. Let him show you that you are beautiful, you are strong, and you were created with a purpose. Take courage in God's love for you and be ready to conquer each day!

January

"Be strong and courageous. Do not be afraid or terrified because of them, for the Lord your God goes with you; he will never leave you nor forsake you."

DEUTERONOMY 31:6 NIV

Doing the Right Thing

If you know of an opportunity to do the right thing today, yet you refrain from doing it, you're guilty of sin.

JAMES 4:17 TPT

Have you ever put off for tomorrow, or next week, or next month something you knew had to be done? While some things on our to-do lists can be relegated to other days, let's not put off the important things that need our attention. What we give our attention to, what we follow through on, are the things by which we are marked and made. Let's not forget our loved ones or our communities in our intentions and actions.

We will never get this time back with our friends and family. We build our lives by our practices and habits, by our connections and relationships. If we can help others today, we should do it. What "right" thing have you been tempted to put off that you can do today? If it requires courage to even face it, ask the Lord for his empowering grace as you take the initiative.

❏ Act of Courage

Instead of putting off an important matter, conversation, or task, make time for it today.

Held by God

Even there Your hand shall lead me,
And Your right hand shall hold me.

PSALM 139:10 NKJV

No matter what you face today, God is with you. In the previous verses of this psalm, David asked the question: "Where can I go from Your Spirit? Or where can I flee from Your presence?" Whether in highest heaven or deepest hell, whether in the driest desert or the fiercest sea, even there God's hand is near, leading and holding.

With the hand of God holding you close, fear does not need to compel you, for his love covers you completely! Take courage and hope in the presence of God, whether you feel the Spirit's nearness or not. You are intimately known by God, and he has not left you, not even for a moment! If you find yourself feeling far from him, read this psalm over and commit it to your heart. Make it your prayer today and keep coming back to it as often as you need it.

☐ Act of Courage

Trust that God is with you wherever you are today, handling what you cannot and helping you as you take the steps you know to take.

Rooted in Peace

Do not lose heart or be afraid when rumors are heard in the land; one rumor comes this year, another the next, rumors of violence in the land and of ruler against ruler.

JEREMIAH 51:46 NIV

It is hard to know what sources to trust these days. It seems wherever we turn, there are differences of opinion about pretty much every topic out there. Let's not allow the rumors based on opinion and conjecture to muddle or confuse us in fear. Let's remain rooted in the persistent peace of Christ which says that even in our suffering we are surrounded by love.

We do not have to face the harsh realities of painful circumstances with positivity. We can accept the truth of what is honestly happening with the challenge that there is goodness to be found even there. Philippians 4:6 states, "Do not be anxious about anything, but in every situation, by prayer and petition, with thanksgiving, present your requests to God." Then, Paul continued, the peace of God will guard our hearts and minds in Christ.

☐ *Act of Courage*

Whenever you feel the tendrils of fear gripping your heart around the news you hear, turn it into prayer!

People of Perseverance

As an example, brothers and sisters,
of suffering and patience,
take the prophets who spoke in the name of the Lord.

JAMES 5:10 NASB

When we need a boost of courage to face our own challenges, it can be helpful to look to the examples of others who have experienced and come through their own. Let's take a look at those who have persevered through trials. Their endurance may give us courage and strength to conquer our own!

Oh, that it were possible to wake up one day and find all our troubles have disappeared! This is not the way of life, however. The messy middle is where our character is refined, and pain cannot be avoided. Instead of running from the suffering we can never escape, let's gather the courage to persist in faith through it, taking it a day at a time with the powerful presence of God as our strength.

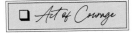

Instead of distracting yourself from the pain in your life, ask God to meet you in the midst of it and to give you the strength to persevere. Look to the testimonies of others who have learned the practice of patient endurance and consider what you can learn from them.

Power of Jesus

> We want all of you and all the people to know that this man was made well by the power of Jesus Christ from Nazareth. You crucified him, but God raised him from the dead. This man was crippled, but he is now well and able to stand here before you because of the power of Jesus.

ACTS 4:10 NCV

This verse was Peter's response to the Sanhedrin, the leaders and teachers of the law in Jerusalem, when they asked what power he invoked to teach and heal others. Instead of cowering as he had before when he denied Jesus three times after Christ was apprehended and before he was crucified, Peter boldly proclaimed the truth of his convictions.

No matter how you have acted in the past whether in fear or self-protection, know that the Holy Spirit empowers you. This is the same Holy Spirit who empowered Peter to boldly proclaim the truth of Jesus Christ to the religious leaders who crucified him. This power and truth is available to you today. The once fearful and ashamed Peter was transformed into a courageously bold leader of the church. As you yield to the Spirit's work in your life, his strength will become your own.

☐ Act of Courage

Ask the Holy Spirit to transform your fear into confident faith.

In All Things

Whether you eat or drink,
or whatever you do,
do all to the glory of God.

1 CORINTHIANS 10:31 ESV

In the freedom of Christ, we can choose what we will eat, drink, and wear, without shame. The law of love is the banner we are under, so let's live according to its standards. As we consider others as well as ourselves and while keeping our consciences clear, the liberty of love frees us from hiding in shame.

We cannot live our lives without regard for how our choices impact others. Our actions ripple into the lives of our family, friends, and communities. We also cannot deflect the responsibility we have to be people of integrity. Without compromising our own convictions and unique personalities, we can live as reflections of God. Let's have the courage to honor God, to honor others, and to honor ourselves. In all things, we have the opportunity to reflect the kindness and goodness God has offered us through Christ. What freedom is ours!

☐ *Act of Courage*

*Whatever you do today, do it intentionally
as an offering to the Lord.*

Even in Doubt

> When he saw the strong wind and the waves, he was
> terrified and began to sink. "Save me, Lord!" he shouted.
> Jesus immediately reached out and grabbed him. "You
> have so little faith," Jesus said. "Why did you doubt me?"
>
> MATTHEW 14:30-31 NLT

Although this verse is often used as an example of what
we shouldn't do, the fact remains, Peter was the only one
brave enough to get out of the boat in the first place.
Without his example we would not know that joining Jesus
and walking on water was even possible!

What if Jesus was not being harsh with Peter, but
rather he was gently and perhaps even a little jokingly
challenging his friend's doubt? He did not berate Peter.
Even in correction, even when Jesus was pointing out
that his friend had no need to doubt, Jesus was kind. He
immediately reached out his hand and caught Peter when
he cried for help. Jesus is trustworthy and faithful even
in our own doubt. Let's not hesitate to cry out to him for
what we need today.

☐ Act of Courage

*Take a step of water-walking courage today and
ask God to catch you if you begin to sink in doubt.*

Stand Strong

Stand firm then, with the belt of truth buckled around your waist, with the breastplate of righteousness in place.

EPHESIANS 6:14 NIV

With truth securely wrapped around us and the breastplate of righteousness covering our hearts, we are able to stand firm in Christ and all that he has already accomplished. Our struggles are not against flesh and blood, as verse eleven of this chapter in Ephesians so clearly says. Let's have the courage to see people with compassion—even those who press our buttons—and understand that the struggles we face are much deeper.

Stand. Stand firm. Stand your ground. This encouragement is given time and time again in this little passage of Scripture. It takes courage to stand when there are forces coming against us. It takes faith to trust that God will not leave us when the storms come, and he says to persist in standing our ground. The ground we are standing on is not that of political power, prestige, or affluent influence. It is the ground of his law of love. Let's never waver from it!

❏ Act of Courage

When you're tempted to insult someone or disparage them even in your own mind, let love cover your thoughts, and then choose to extend mercy and compassion instead.

Hope-filled Trust

"At last the fulfillment of the age has come! It is time for the realm of God's kingdom to be experienced in its fullness! Turn your lives back to God and put your trust in the hope-filled gospel!"

MARK 1:15 TPT

Jesus' message of hope was clearly displayed through his ministry. Markedly, this verse was proclaimed at the beginning of his ministry. Through Jesus' teachings, healings, and lifestyle we clearly see the expansion of God's kingdom. Through his loving acts, there is fullness of life for each of us.

The Holy Spirit, who is given to all who believe in Christ, is the one who teaches us the ways of Christ's kingdom and who reminds us of all he said and did (John 14:26). When we turn our lives to God, offering him ourselves and putting our trust in the hope-filled gospel, there is wonderful freedom for our hearts in his love! There is more wisdom and goodness to discover in the realms of his glory than we can ever imagine, and the Holy Spirit opens our spiritual eyes with revelation.

☐ *Act of Courage*

Put your trust in God today and ask the Holy Spirit to teach you the ways of Christ.

Strengthened by Prayer

You, beloved, building yourselves up on your most holy
faith, praying in the Holy Spirit.

JUDE 1:20 NKJV

How do you build yourself up in faith? Strong faith is
accomplished by fastening your heart to the love of
God, receiving the mercy of Jesus, and by praying every
moment in the Spirit. Spiritual strength is found in your
connection to God. It cannot be measured by another's
perception of you. It has nothing to do with how many
physical resources you have.

Jesus said when you abide in him you will bear his fruit
(John 15). Your power comes from the source of love
himself. Strengthen yourself in him by turning your
attention to him and surrendering to his love. Pray in all
circumstances whether brushing your teeth or meeting
with people in a boardroom. Give him your cares, for he
cares for you! You will find your courage in the advocacy of
the Holy Spirit. You are seen, known, and loved. Press into
prayer today and build bricks of faith within the structure
of your life.

☐ *Act of Courage*

*Make a practice of prayer today by using physical cues
such as whenever you go into your kitchen,
open a door, or brush your teeth.*

Real Love

This is how we know what real love is:
Jesus gave his life for us.
So we should give our lives for our brothers and sisters.

1 JOHN 3:16 NCV

When we help others in need, we demonstrate the love of God living in us. Jesus withheld nothing so we could know the extravagant extent of the Father's love for us. When we practice generosity with our love, our lives, and our resources, we affirm that our trust is not in what we acquire but in the overwhelming and endless love of God.

Let's not be stingy with our encouragement, our affection, or our time. Instead, let's put into practice the kingdom value of generosity and thereby partnering with God's heart. Let's not forget to go to God first and fill up on his affection for us. From a place of fullness we can overflow into the lives of others without resentment or depletion.

☐ Act of Courage

Ask God what he thinks of you today, and then ask him to give you the lens of his love for others. Act from that place.

Find Your Joy

"How ecstatic you can be when people insult and persecute you and speak all kinds of cruel lies about you because of your love for me!"

MATTHEW 5:11 TPT

I don't know about you, but it is not natural for me to find joy in others insulting me. We want to belong, and we don't want to be ridiculed for who we are. Yet Jesus says when others mistreat us and criticize us because of our love for him, our heavenly reward is great. What joy awaits us!

Let's keep in mind that Jesus was explicitly saying that when we are persecuted for *doing what is right*, we should delight in it. However, we should not conflate unjust persecution with accountability. There is a time and a place for criticism that is well warranted. Let us remain humble in love in all things, and we can find our joy as we courageously face whatever may come!

☐ *Act of Courage*

*Ask God to change your mindset over a trial
in which you have been facing great discouragement.
Dare to look for the goodness and joy in the mess!*

Small Seeds of Faith

"Because of your meager faith; for truly I say to you, if you have faith the size of a mustard seed, you will say to this mountain, 'Move from here to there,' and it will move; and nothing will be impossible for you."

MATTHEW 17:20 NASB

The mustard seed is one of the smallest seeds planted in the ground. Though tiny, when fully grown it produces a large tree where birds can nest. Though our faith may be small, Jesus told us that it is still powerful enough to move mountains. What a marvelous mystery!

It takes courage to take God at his Word and to trust he will be faithful to his promises. Yet whether we believe him or not, he cannot change his nature. He is faithful because it is in his character. He loves because he is made up of love. May we trust that Jesus' Words are as applicable in our lives as they were to the first hearers. Jesus said that with God all things are possible. Let's stretch our faith no matter how meager it is and put it completely in him!

☐ Act of Courage

Stretch your faith in prayer and action today in one specific way.

Simply Believe

Overhearing what they said, Jesus said to the ruler of
the synagogue, "Do not fear, only believe."

MARK 5:36 ESV

It is important that we take the context of this verse into
consideration. There was a synagogue leader whose
daughter was gravely ill, and he asked Jesus to come to
his house to heal her. While they were on their way, people
from Jairus' house arrived and informed them that the
daughter had died. Today's verse is Jesus' statement to the
desperate father.

Have you ever been desperate for God's help? When others
step in and confirm your greatest fears, you have two
choices: you can be overcome by them, or you can listen
for Jesus' voice. He will not always say the same thing, but
his voice always carries authority and brings peace. Lean
in to hear his whisper, and don't let the forces of fear drag
you or your hope away. Jesus will go with you, and you
have only to rely on him.

☐ Act of Courage

When you are overwhelmed by what you are hearing
from others in the world, listen for Jesus' voice
and believe he speaks truth.

Hope in the Waiting

We wait in hope for the LORD;
he is our help and our shield.

PSALM 33:20 NIV

The space between hope and fulfillment right in the middle of the worst tension can be trying. There may be different phases to your waiting seasons, and that's okay. No matter where you find yourself today whether you are full of hope or leaning more toward despair, instead of looking to the promise itself, look to the Promise Keeper.

The wraparound presence of God is your strength and shield. Ask God to give you eyes to see where he is already working miracles of mercy in your life. Ask him to speak hope into your heart through whatever means necessary. Take a walk outside looking for evidence of God's faithfulness in nature. Call an old friend and catch up. Read a favorite passage from a book. You can take courage in the waiting because God is with you in it, and he is not finished working out the details of your story.

☐ *Act of Courage*

Read today's verse in multiple translations declaring it over your life, your family, and your community. Use it to intercede for others.

Our Great Confidence

God has given both his promise and his oath. These two things are unchangeable because it is impossible for God to lie. Therefore, we who have fled to him for refuge can have great confidence as we hold to the hope that lies before us.

HEBREWS 6:18 NLT

Not only do we find strength in the faithfulness of God, but there is comfort for our hurting souls as well. Is there an area where you need the comforting embrace of God's love? Hide yourself in the refuge of his heart; in that place you will be empowered to seize what is already available to you—an unshakeable hope.

It is impossible for God to lie. He will not turn his back on those who look to him for help. Lean into the presence of the One who is for you. The Father runs to meet you when you turn to him, and the Comforter wraps his royal robes around you. You are so very loved. May the refuge of his presence be a balm to your soul and courage for your day.

☐ *Act of Courage*

Declare the promises of God over your life today and direct your attention to his faithfulness.

Dawn of Love's Light

Let the sunrise of your love end our dark night. Break through our clouded dawn again! Only you can satisfy our hearts, filling us with songs of joy to the end of our days.

PSALM 90:14 TPT

In the dark nights of the soul, it can feel like the greatest fight to hold on to the hope of a new day dawning. Even though we know the sun will rise again, the oppressiveness of our pain can cloud the hope of the relief we so long for. It takes courage to get through the long, dark night when sleep evades us.

May the sunrise of God's love end your dark night and bring with it the dawning of the relief, the joy, and the peace you have been longing for. Even in the midst of the greatest storms of life, Christ's peace is present. His love is everlasting, and it reaches you. May you experience the superior satisfaction of your heart in the balm of his affection and care for you.

❏ Act of Courage

Sing a song that brings you joy,
even if you need to do it defiantly!

He Shows You

> "Indeed, for this reason I have allowed you to remain, in order to show you My power and in order to proclaim My name throughout the earth."
>
> Exodus 9:16 NASB

God shows his power to both the willing and the unwilling. Take courage in his strength. Listen to his voice and follow where he leads. It is much better to witness his power from inside the embrace of his favor than it is to resist his truth and witness it on the other side!

Whatever you are getting ready to face, may you seek God first and foremost. May you know the empowering grace he gives through his Spirit to strengthen you from the inside out. What you are seeking you will find, so be sure to look for wisdom. Seek out truth and stand for justice. Have courage to embrace the Lord, and trust that he will show you his power.

☐ Act of Courage

Listen for the voice of the Lord and respond to what he says.

Remember

I speak over my heartbroken soul, "Take courage.
Remember when you used to be right out front leading
the procession of praise when the great crowd of
worshipers gathered to go into the presence of the
Lord? You shouted with joy as the sound of passionate
celebration filled the air and the joyous multitude of
lovers honored the festival of the Lord!"

PSALM 42:4 TPT

Sometimes what we need in order to garner courage is to
remind ourselves of what we've already walked through. What
joys have been ours? What challenges have we already faced
and come through to times of triumph and celebration?

Don't just remember the hard times, but also remember
the good. Take courage as you recall the passion you felt in
the presence of the Lord. Remember how he spoke to you,
the deep joy of being fully known and accepted in his love.
Remember the relief you found in the company of others.
And as you remember, dare your soul to hope. You are not
finished yet, and there is more goodness to discover in the
land of the living.

❑ *Act of Courage*

*Time to think back to a time when you were filled with
joy, peace, and overflowing awe. When you do remember
these special times, speak courage over your soul.*

Look to the Comforter

"I—I am the one who comforts you.
Who are you that you should fear humans who die,
or a son of man who is given up like grass?"

ISAIAH 51:12 CSB

When we have deeply rooted confidence in God, the Creator and our Comforter, what reason do we have to fear another person? Every human faces the same decay. No matter how powerful or charismatic someone may be, they will face their mortality just as we all will. They cannot elude death no matter how hard they try.

Knowing your life is ultimately in the hands of God and not others, how can you approach life differently? Is there an area where fear has kept you from taking a stand or living in the integrity of your passions? May you experience the liberating love of God today through fellowship with the Spirit of Christ, and may you have the courage to face your fears, knowing your Comforter is near.

☐ Act of Courage

Don't let someone else's attempts to control you through fear keep you on a path that is not yours. Stay true to who God has created you to be.

Peace that Overcomes

> "These things I have spoken to you, that in Me you may have peace. In the world you will have tribulation; but be of good cheer, I have overcome the world."
>
> JOHN 16:33 NKJV

Jesus' life was not without its difficulties. Why would we expect ours to be smooth sailing? A good life is not a life without suffering. It is one that is filled with loyal love and peace no matter the circumstances. Even when our hearts are trembling within us, we are not alone in facing any trial. We are never alone.

Jesus warned his disciples he would not be with them forever. He told them he would lay down his life. However they took it at the time, confused or skimming over the truth behind his words, they were confronted with the reality when he was crucified. What a comfort it must have been later to discover the true meaning behind his Words. Jesus had warned them even if they had not understood. He offers us peace of heart today. We have his Spirit to minister to us with comfort, courage, and restoration when we need it most.

☐ Act of Courage

Instead of being discouraged by challenges that arise seemingly out of nowhere, remind yourself that God is not surprised, and he is with you in it. He offers all you need!

Trustworthy Strength

Some trust in chariots and some in horses,
but we trust in the name of the Lord our God.

PSALM 20:7 NIV

The weapons of this world will fail at times, and no amount of armor can keep us safe from the threat of powerful forces. Where is our trust in times of uncertainty? Where do we place our confidence? Do we trust in ourselves and our own scrappiness, or do we trust that the Lord will conquer what we cannot move an inch on our own?

Jesus Christ is victorious. He has already defeated the grave and has set us free in his love. His invitation is open for everyone. May our hearts, our lives, and our very beings be rooted in the steadfast love of God that cannot be overcome by the forces of darkness. Let's put our trust in the one who never fails!

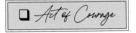

☐ *Act of Courage*

When you are moved by worry today, before you jump into action, turn your attention to the Lord and put your trust in him. Then partner with him as you go about your day.

Encouraged by Support

When the believers were alerted we were coming, they came out to meet us at the Forum of Appius while we were still a great distance from Rome. Another group met us at the Three Taverns. When Paul saw the believers, his heart was greatly encouraged and he thanked God.

ACTS 28:15 TPT

Sometimes we cannot conjure courage on our own. Spiritual support is wonderful, and words of encouragement are great, but embodied support in people showing up is invaluable. When was the last time someone's presence brought relief and encouragement? As you consider what this meant for you, is there someone who is struggling that you could support in the same way?

Showing up for those we care about cannot be overstated. It is in the solidarity of friendship, of physical help, and of the encouragement of knowing we are not alone when our souls can find incredible amounts of courage. May we not neglect the important and tangible work of meeting those who need to know they are not alone.

❑ Act of Courage

Show up in a tangible way even if you cannot physically be with them. Call, send flowers, or be thoughtful in some other way for a friend who is struggling.

Share Your Story

> "We cannot stop telling about everything we have seen and heard."

ACTS 4:20 NLT

Peter and John were brought before a council of Jewish leaders, religious scholars, and elders of Jerusalem. After questioning them about the power and authority they were operating under in their ministries—healing people, mostly—the council commanded them to never again teach the people or to speak using the name of Jesus. In the face of unknown consequences, both Peter and John refused. In today's verse from the book of Acts, they succinctly said they were compelled by the ministry of Christ to continue.

If Peter and John could withstand the threats of the Sanhedrin, can't we stand strong in the truth of what God has also called us to do? May we know the limitless grace and kindness God has shown toward us through Christ (Ephesians 2:7). May we live with wholehearted abandon to the overwhelming love of God which transforms our mourning into dancing!

☐ Act of Courage

Don't back down with the convictions that are rooted in God's love. Stand strong and follow your passion!

Active Love

Little children, let us not love in word or speech,
but in action and in truth.

1 John 3:18 CSB

It takes boldness to not simply say we love others, but to follow through in loving care and action toward them. The verse in 1 John that follows today's verse goes on to say it is our actions that show we belong to the truth. Our confidence in standing before God is in the love we are living out right now. Let's humble ourselves before our good God. As he lavishes his love on us, we have his example to follow.

We do not reflect Christ well if we do not love one another. When we share our hearts, our resources, and our lives with others we connect not only to each other but to God. We are all unique reflections of God's face. Why then would we treat anyone as if they are less than anyone else? Let's be people who show our love in meaningful and practical ways!

☐ *Act of Courage*

*Instead of using your words to express love today,
show it in tangible expressions and actions.*

Guarded by God

> He is a shield to those who walk in integrity,
> guarding the paths of justice and watching over the way
> of his saints.
> Then you will understand righteousness
> and justice and equity, every good path.
>
> PROVERBS 2:7-9 ESV

When we follow the ways of God, he becomes like a personal bodyguard protecting us as we choose what is right. There is a wealth of wisdom in the storehouses of our God! There are limitless riches of knowledge hidden in him. May we become pursuers of truth, justice, and righteousness. May we walk in his mercy all the days of our lives.

With God as our guard, we will not avoid the limitations that life places on us, but we will know the surpassing goodness of his peace, his fellowship, and his solutions. The relationship of Spirit to spirit is the most fulfilling one we will know in this life. There is so much life in his presence. There is so much peace in his ways! Let's never stop following him, for he is better than any other!

☐ *Act of Courage*

*Trust God to handle what you cannot foresee
or control as you follow his directives.*

Passionate Pursuit

With passion I pursue and cling to you.
Because I feel your grip on my life,
I keep my soul close to your heart.

PSALM 63:8 TPT

In the verses leading up to David's statement here, he said, "I lie awake each night thinking of you and reflecting on how you help me like a father. I sing through the night under your splendor-shadow, offering up to you my songs of delight and joy!" The dark of night can often bring our fears to life in our minds. Instead of focusing on these, what if we followed the lead of King David?

In moments of fear, let's teach our hearts to turn to the Lord. Let's remember how he has helped us like a father. Let's think about the goodness of God. Let's sing songs in the darkness, offering delight and joy. And even when all we have is a faint melody, let's hum it all the same. There is power in praise, and it compels us to passionately pursue God's heart.

☐ Act of Courage

The next time you lie awake at night, think of this psalm and turn your attention to the Lord.

Confidence of Integrity

Our conscience testifies that we have conducted ourselves in the world, and especially in our relations with you, with integrity and godly sincerity. We have done so, relying not on worldly wisdom but on God's grace.

2 CORINTHIANS 1:12 NIV

When we act in integrity, living for God's values and keeping ourselves aboveboard, we have nothing to hide when others throw accusations our way. The truth will always be found out, so let's be sure to be people who are trustworthy and true. A web of lies catches the deceiver, but a truth-teller stands unencumbered.

It is no small thing to boldly stand for truth when it would be easier to let things slide. However, our integrity is made or broken in the decisions we make. Let's be brave enough to choose honesty even when it is the harder way. There is grace enough to strengthen us in our resolve!

☐ *Act of Courage*

When faced with an opportunity to compromise, let's stand in the truth of our convictions, leading with sincerity and love.

Spirit Life

*This is what God made us for, and he has given us the
Spirit to be a guarantee for this new life.*

2 CORINTHIANS 5:5 NCV

For what exactly has God has created us? It is to be
"clothed with our heavenly home" (2 Corinthians 5:4).
Paul reminded us of the knowledge of our mortality in the
beginning of this chapter. When we are faced with the
limitations of our lives, let us not give in to despair. Our lives
do not end when our bodies fail us. There is an eternal hope
in the glory of Christ's kingdom in which we get to share.

The Holy Spirit is our guarantee for this new life we await.
The breath of God's very own Spirit gives life, hope, love,
joy, peace, and strength into our inner beings. This is why
Paul continued in verse six, "so we always have courage."
We have courage because of the companionship of his
Spirit which never leaves us!

❑ *Act of Courage*

*Spend time in prayer asking the Holy Spirit to fill you
with courage, hope, and vision for his kingdom.*

Possibilities of Faith

Jesus answered and said to them, "Truly I say to you, if you have faith and do not doubt, you will not only do what was done to the fig tree, but even if you say to this mountain, 'Be taken up and cast into the sea,' it will happen."

MATTHEW 21:21 NASB

On a walk with his disciples, Jesus, hungry—maybe a little hangry, it appears—approached a fig tree to eat its fruit. When he saw there was no fruit to pick, he spoke to the tree, declaring it would never bear fruit again. The tree then shriveled up before their eyes. At seeing this the disciples were astonished, and they asked how Jesus was able to do it. In today's verse, we have Jesus' response.

There is power in our faith, coupled with our action. If we truly believe the authority of Christ is also the power in which we walk, then we can do the greater things that Jesus spoke of when he said, "Truly I say to you, the one who believes in Me...greater works than these he will do" (John 14:12). Do we truly believe we can partner with God in faith and see miracles come to life around us? Let's be intentional with our words, for they are powerful.

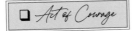

❏ Act of Courage

Consider how you can stretch yourself today and make a purposeful declaration of faith.

Multiplied Grace

May grace and peace be multiplied to you in the knowledge of God and of Jesus our Lord.

2 PETER 1:2 ESV

God does not give small doses of grace to some and larger to others. He offers the same cascading grace to cover each of us. Though our needs are different, his grace is the same. It is more than enough to meet us where we're at. Today, no matter what you are facing or what you are lacking, may grace and peace be multiplied to you!

Look to Jesus now. Read through his words laid out in the gospels. Go over your journals or just think back to a time when God's faithfulness was clear to you. Sometimes we get a clearer vision of mercy's work through hindsight. As you remember what God has already done, may grace and peace rise up to lift your soul to meet today's challenges and opportunities. God is with you still, and he will not leave you. May his strength become your own as you lean on him and trust his loyal nature.

Offer grace to others when they disappoint you or fail to meet your expectations. Let them off the hook and receive the same grace from God today.

February

God did not give us
a spirit that makes us afraid
but a spirit of power
and love and self-control.

2 TIMOTHY 1:7 NCV

Where Mercy Meets Us

Return to your rest, O my soul,
For the LORD has dealt bountifully with you.
For You have delivered my soul from death,
My eyes from tears,
And my feet from falling.

PSALM 116:7-8 NKJV

When we recognize the areas in which God has already delivered us, it gives us tangible examples of mercy's imprint on our lives. What God has done, he will do again. What peace there is in knowing God is a loving and faithful father. He will never turn away from those who look to him for help.

Even in the midst of our deepest darkness, in the pits of our own shame, fear, and pain, his loving light meets us. He surrounds us with songs of deliverance. He covers us with the embrace of his love. He never leaves or forsakes us. He is with us in the dirt, and he is with us when we're flying high. He is with us. Mercy is with us.

☐  *Act of Courage*

*When you feel overwhelmed today,
remind your soul that God is near,
and he will not leave you alone.*

Hope for All

"He will not falter or be discouraged
till he establishes justice on earth.
In his teaching the islands will put their hope."

ISAIAH 42:4 NIV

It takes unfailing courage to not become discouraged when faced with the unexpected challenges of life. God will follow through on every promise he has made, though not in our timelines and often not in ways we imagine. He is better than our understanding, and he is wiser than the most astute minds this world has known.

Jesus is the hope for all nations. He is the hope of those who are vastly different than us just as much as he is the hope for our own communities. There are no walls or separations in his lavish love. May we have the courage to refuse to erect walls that Jesus came to demolish. No one is more worthy than another for his love. We can hold on to his promises and also offer compassion and practical mercy to others while we do. Let's look to Christ in all we do.

☐ Act of Courage

Be kind to someone you would
normally avoid interacting with.

Admit Your Reality

> Jesus said to him, "What do you mean 'if'? If you are able to believe, all things are possible to the believer." When he heard this, the boy's father cried out with tears, saying, "I do believe, Lord; help my little faith!"
>
> MARK 9:23-24 TPT

The father of a tormented child desperately wanted to believe Jesus could set his boy free and heal him. Even so, he was honest with where he was at personally: "I do believe, Lord; help my little faith!" In other versions, this phrase is translated as, "Help my unbelief!" He offered his little faith and still asked for God to help the parts of him that struggled to believe.

We don't have to pretend with God. It takes courage to admit what we don't know and to also remain open to possibilities that are better than our expectations. When we dare to ask Jesus for help, he is more than able to give it. Let's not use faith as a weapon against one another but rather have the courage to bolster each other in prayer and support. May we offer our honest prayers, for God sees our hearts in any case!

☐ Act of Courage

Admit the reality of your heart today,
even while asking for God to help you grow in faith.

Safe Place

You have been a refuge for me,
A tower of strength against the enemy.

PSALM 61:3 NASB

The Lord is not a small safe place to run into; he is a
"paradise of protection" to us (TPT). He lifts us above
the commotion and sets us securely in the safety of his
wraparound presence. He is our tower of strength, a
stronghold and a refuge. His peace fills us even when we
are surrounded by the enemy.

Let's run into the arms of our good Father today. Let's not
stay away for he never rejects us when we turn to him.
When we are weak and overwhelmed by life, we can find
rest in the glory of his presence. In this place, peace is our
plentiful portion. There is restoration and rejuvenation
for our souls. Even when we struggle to find our footing,
he is the firm foundation beneath our feet. Let's turn our
attention to him whenever we feel the earth or our lives
trembling.

❑ Act of Courage

*When you feel overwhelmed today, find a physical space
where you can ground yourself in the goodness of God,
even if just for a few minutes at a time.*

Trustworthy Judge

When he was insulted, he did not insult in return;
when he suffered, he did not threaten but entrusted
himself to the one who judges justly.

1 PETER 2:23 CSB

It takes an incredible amount of courageous trust to not
return insults with insults or to repay abusers with physical
harm. When we put our lives in God's hands, we trust him
to exert his justice over us. His ways are better, and his
perception is clearer than ours. If left to our own devices,
we would probably adopt the "eye for an eye" ideology.
And yet Jesus showed us another, better way.

When we suffer, our worth is not diminished. When others
wrongly accuse or abuse us, it is not a reflection of our
identity, but of theirs. Instead of seeking revenge which
may never satisfy, let's trust God to be their judge. Let's
allow mercy's power to relieve our need for retribution.
Jesus did not abuse or threaten, so let's never make
excuses for it. Accountability is a worthwhile endeavor, but
revenge is not.

❑ Act of Courage

*When someone insults, ridicules, or causes you pain today,
forgive them and let it go.*

Greater Purpose

"Be of good courage, and let us be courageous for our people, and for the cities of our God, and may the Lord do what seems good to him."

2 SAMUEL 10:12 ESV

When we offer mutual support and help to others, both sides benefit. When we know we can count on others in the same way we offer ourselves, there is security and greater courage to face whatever may come! In the solidarity and power of partnership, we are able to do more than we could while trying to go it alone.

In all we do, let's keep a vision of the bigger picture. Our actions not only affect our own lives, but we can influence, inspire, and uplift others in the process. Let's be intentional about how we can sow courage into our communities. Let's partner with others in pursuing what God has paved the way for, and let's do it all for the greater good!

☐ Act of Courage

Instead of trying to move ahead on your own, think of someone you could potentially partner with to make a greater impact.

Victorious Truth

You belong to God, my dear children. You have already
won a victory over those people, because the Spirit
who lives in you is greater than the spirit who lives
in the world.

1 JOHN 4:4 NLT

We belong to God like children belong to their parents.
As we get to know him, we can tell truth from deception.
When others claim to speak for God, but they don't
represent his character—his love, his mercy, his justice, or
his peace—we will be able to tell. Knowing God's heart,
his intentions, and the timbre of his voice, we are able
to represent him well. We cannot claim to know God by
simply abiding by laws and rules. We must press into the
relationship of Spirit to spirit.

There is victory in the truth of God's liberating love. There
is freedom in his overwhelmingly good and true nature.
The gospel of Christ is the good news of our redemption.
May we find our triumph and success in his finished work!

☐ *Act of Courage*

*Spend time with the Lord today in prayer and meditation
on his Word and ask him to reveal himself in a deeper way
through fellowship with his Spirit.*

Strength in Solidarity

Refuse to give in to him, by standing strong in your faith. You know that your Christian family all over the world is having the same kinds of suffering.

1 PETER 5:9 NCV

Sometimes, the mere knowledge we are not the only ones who struggle or suffer is enough to bolster our courage to persevere. Whatever you are going through, know that you are not alone. There are others experiencing the same pain. Have you ever felt like you were uniquely struggling, only to find relief in hearing someone else expressing that they experience the same struggle?

Solidarity can do a lot to encourage us in endurance. When we know others have gone through deep valleys of darkness and made it through to the other side, we are able to garner hope to continue. May we find strength in knowing the communal aspect of struggle and keep pressing on in faith!

Share a struggle you are experiencing with a trusted friend. If that is not enough, look for a support group that can help you in your time of need.

Peacemakers

The fruit of righteousness is sown in peace by those who make peace.

JAMES 3:18 NKJV

In a world full of conflict, it is more courageous to pursue peace than it is to pick a fight. One of the fruits of the Spirit is peace. Let's look through the evidence we are given of the Spirit's work in our lives in Galatians 5: love, joy, peace, longsuffering, kindness, goodness, faithfulness, gentleness, and self-control.

Notice within the fruits of the Spirit listed, there is no charisma, wealth, heavy-handedness, or controlling others. Let's be people of peace who are patient, kind, full of goodness, faithfulness, self-control, and joy. Though the powerful may intimidate with their resources, God does no such thing. Let's promote peace whenever possible, extending mercy instead of vengeance. This is the way of the cross.

☐ *Act of Courage*

Instead of jumping to conclusions and fighting someone because of it, slow down and seek to understand them. That is the way to pursue peace.

Keep Loving Others

These are his commands: that we continually place our trust in the name of his Son, Jesus Christ, and that we keep loving one another, just as he has commanded us. For all who obey his commands find their lives joined in union with him, and he lives and flourishes in them.

1 JOHN 3:23-24 TPT

Only the brave continue to keep their hearts open and to lean into love when they have experienced disappointment, heartbreak, and loss. It is a vital and revolutionary act to choose to keep loving one another in the midst of all of our humanity.

Jesus said that the greatest commandment, the essence of all the Law and the Prophets, is to, "Love the Lord your God with every passion of your heart, with all the energy of your being, and with every thought that is within you...You must love your friend in the same way you love yourself" (Matthew 22:37, 39). Let's keep first things first and be courageous enough to make love our greatest priority.

Forgive someone who has hurt you.

Faith Fighters

Fight the good fight of the faith. Take hold of
the eternal life to which you were called when you
made your good confession in the presence
of many witnesses.

1 TIMOTHY 6:12 NIV

The same writer who said, "your fight is not against flesh
and blood," is the one who encourages Timothy to keep
fighting the good fight of faith. If this fight is not against
others, what is it? Are we to fight the air? Paul said in 1
Corinthians 9:26, "I do not fight like a boxer beating the
air." He continued in verse 27: "No, I strike a blow to my
body and make it my slave so that after I have preached to
others, I myself will not be disqualified for the prize."

With humility, self-control, and compassion, we do not run
aimlessly. Taking hold of the eternal life to which we were
called is keeping faith at the forefront. When we live by
the values of Christ's kingdom, we reflect the power of his
love. So, let's fight the good fight of faith, but let's do it by
taking ownership of our choices, controlling our reactions,
and remaining humble in the love of Christ!

☐ Act of Courage

*Resist the urge to fight others today and instead fight to
keep yourself clothed in love!*

Chosen

You are a chosen people, a royal priesthood, a holy nation, a people for God's own possession, so that you may proclaim the excellencies of Him who has called you out of darkness into His marvelous light.

1 PETER 2:9 NASB

What courage comes from confidence in our identities as sons and daughters of the living God! Before we could choose whom we would serve in this life, before we could utter intelligible words, God chose us as his own. Every person who comes to him has been drawn by his merciful light.

We are not members of an exclusive club but of an ever-expanding family. Let's never shut the door to others, for God welcomes all who come with the same loyal love we find for ourselves. Let's never stop telling of the glorious wonders of his love! His mercy is an open embrace for all to enter in and be covered by its power.

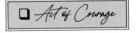
☐ Act of Courage

Share with someone today what freedom you have found in Christ's love.

Lifted Up

He replied to them, "Who among you, if he had a sheep
that fell into a pit on the Sabbath, wouldn't take hold
of it and lift it out? A person is worth far more than
a sheep; so it is lawful to do what is good on
the Sabbath."

MATTHEW 12:11-12 CSB

There is no law against showing kindness to others. When
we put boundaries on our own acts of compassion and
mercy, we misunderstand the love of God. It is always
appropriate to do good even when others judge us for
it. Let's make sure our own hearts are being led by the
limitless mercy of Christ and not being ruled by the
regulations of people who dictate when, where, and how
we can show kindness.

How many struggling people have you passed without
a second thought? Surely we cannot help everyone we
meet, but compassion can be shown regardless. Have the
courage to do good today even if you aren't sure how
others will view it. Jesus is always on the side of mercy!

☐ *Act of Courage*

When you see someone in need today, offer them
something, whether it's a word of kindness,
a meal, or simply your attention.

Hope for Today

Whatever was written in former days was written for our instruction, that through endurance and through the encouragement of the Scriptures we might have hope.

ROMANS 15:4 ESV

There is wisdom in the ages that have preceded us. Let's not forget to look to the experience of those who have gone before us in finding encouragement, hope, and a path forward for our own healing, restoration, and endurance.

If you have a favorite book of the Bible, read some of it today. If you don't know where to begin, perhaps read a proverb. If you are feeling overwhelmed by life, read a psalm. If you need encouragement to keep going, Paul's letters may be of help. If you struggle to know what to focus on right now, look to the words and life of Jesus. May the Spirit guide your heart and reveal the nature and nurture of the Father in deeper ways as you meditate on Scripture today.

❑ Act of Courage

Memorize a verse today to come back to throughout your week when you need a bit of courage or redirection in hope.

Power of Relationship

By his divine power, God has given us everything we
need for living a godly life. We have received all of
this by coming to know him, the one who called us to
himself by means of his marvelous glory and excellence.

2 PETER 1:3 NLT

We do not gain favor with the Lord by doing more. We
cannot earn his love, nor can we lose his mercy or kindness
by our mistakes. There is no need to press for perfection
when he already accepts us as we are. Life in Christ is not
about following a list of rules and regulations, proving how
holy we are. It is a living, fluid relationship with the Father
through Christ who transforms our very lives!

Think of your closest friends, your most trusted mentors
in life, and those with whom you spend the most time.
How does their influence affect your choices and lifestyle?
Relationship with the Spirit of God can be the greatest
transformative agent in your life if you will give your time
and attention to getting to know him more. There is beauty
and goodness beyond imagining in his wonderful fellowship!

☐ *Act of Courage*

*Ask the Holy Spirit to draw you into deeper fellowship
with the kingdom of God today, revealing the heart of
the Father and the friendship of Christ.*

Keep Going

I can do all things through Christ,
because he gives me strength.

PHILIPPIANS 4:13 NCV

God has not left us on our own to waste away in the chaos of our troubles. He does not leave us when our pain feels like too great a weight to bear. He is closer than our own breath, wrapping us in the comfort of his Spirit's embrace.

Whatever challenges you face today, know that Christ is with you. He offers you the strength of his partnership and power. Remember Jesus' words in Matthew 11: "Come to me, all of you who are tired and have heavy loads, and I will give you rest...The burden that I ask you to accept is easy; the load I give you to carry is light" (verses 28, 30). He relieves the weight of our burdens and offers us a light load in return. Let's take him up on his offer today and also echo Paul's words in 2 Corinthians 12:10: "When I am weak, then I am truly strong."

☐ Act of Courage

Partner with Christ and keep going,
persevering with his strength as your own.

Promise of Breakthrough

Strengthen those who are discouraged.
Energize those who feel defeated.

ISAIAH 35:3 TPT

This passage of Scripture continues in a powerful way, "Say to the anxious and fearful, 'Be strong and never afraid. Look; here comes your God! He is breaking through to give you victory!'" How do we encourage those who are feeling defeated? By reminding them of the promises of God!

Jesus said in John 10:10, "I have come to give you everything in abundance, more than you expect—life in its fullness until you overflow!" He is our Good Shepherd, and he will never leave us. The promise of abundant life is not in how much wealth we garner or how easy our lives may seem. It is in the abundance of peace, joy, love, and the other wonderful fruits of the Spirit's work in our lives! If you are feeling discouraged, know that there is breakthrough coming for you. Though the night seems like it may never end, morning always comes and with it, the hope of a new day!

☐ *Act of Courage*

Encourage someone who is struggling today.

Reasons to Rest

The LORD is my light and my salvation—
so why should I be afraid?
The LORD is my fortress, protecting me from danger,
so why should I tremble?

PSALM 27:1 NLT

With God as our mighty defense, our Savior, and our restorer, no one can take away what he offers. Even when our bodies fail, his love never does. Even when our knees tremble and our hearts lurch, his peace is palpably plentiful. When we feel the tendrils of fear creeping into our consciousness, let's invite the peace of God as we breathe in his presence. He is here now. He is near always.

When there is no good news to be heard, he is still good. When there are endless rumors of corruption, greed, and wickedness, he is still merciful, kind, powerful, and true. Let's remind our souls of his unchanging nature, of his limitless power, and of his overwhelming love as often as our hearts need the reminder.

☐ *Act of Courage*

Remind yourself of God's faithful and loving nature whenever you are bogged down by fear today.

Precious Assurances

> Through these he gave us the very great and precious promises. With these gifts you can share in God's nature, and the world will not ruin you with its evil desires.
>
> 2 PETER 1:4 NCV

Through Christ, we experience and share in the divine nature of God. His powerful love transforms us from the inside out, making us reflective images of his wonderful nature. Let's give ourselves to knowing Christ more than we do pleasing our own palates. He is the pure and priceless likeness of the Father in human form. Let's look to his example more than we do any other, for he was sent by God to show us what the Father's heart looks like.

Christ has made us partners to share in his character. Let's be sure to listen to what he says, to have the courage to hold on to faith and walk it out, and to press into the fellowship of his Spirit. God will never go back on his promises, so let's take him at his word and walk in the confidence of his faithfulness.

Remind yourself of the promises of Christ. Pick one promise of Christ from the Scriptures and write it down in a place you will see it.

Listen to Wisdom

Out in the open wisdom calls aloud,
she raises her voice in the public square;
on top of the wall she cries out,
at the city gate she makes her speech.

PROVERBS 1:20-21 NIV

We do well when we take God's wisdom to heart. First
Corinthians 1:25 says, "The foolishness of God is wiser than
human wisdom, and the weakness of God is stronger than
human strength." As we trust God, following his Word and
instructions even when we don't quite understand at the
time, we will see God's wisdom is better than the world's.

God consistently chooses the weak and foolish things
of the world to shame those who are wise in their own
eyes. There is no one he can't use, and there is nothing he
withholds from willing and yielded hearts. Remain humble,
recognizing that you don't know better than God so you
can learn from him. Follow the lead of wisdom today
and lay down your pride so you grow in love and true
understanding.

❏ *Act of Courage*

*Admit to yourself that you don't know what you don't
know and be willing to change your mind
when presented with better information.*

God Sees Me

She named the Lord who spoke to her: "You are El-roi,"
for she said, "In this place, have I actually seen the one
who sees me?"

GENESIS 16:13 CSB

In other translations of this text, it is clear that Hagar was
awed by the Lord who encountered her in her greatest
need. The Lord spoke to her, prophesying her future and
the future of her descendants. Though she may have felt
disregarded by the people around her, including Sarah and
Abraham, God met her in a powerful moment of kindness.
It is her response that shows her wonder: "You are the God
who sees me...I have now seen the One who sees me" (NIV).

Have you had an encounter with the love of Christ which
has made you feel seen? There are no mysteries to God.
He knows your past, your present, and your future. He is
close to you. If you need encouragement from him, do not
hesitate to ask! He is ready to speak words of life into your
heart today.

☐ Act of Courage

*Ask God to speak to you in a way that
makes you feel seen and known by him.*

Prisoners of Hope

> "As for you also, because of the blood of My covenant with you, I have set your prisoners free from the waterless pit. Return to the stronghold, you prisoners who have the hope; This very day I am declaring that I will restore double to you."
>
> ZECHARIAH 9:11-12 NASB

God will never go back on his covenantal promises. Often what we lose in captivity, God restores in greater measure. Have you gone through a time of great loss? Have you been struggling to know if you will experience the restoration of freedom and rest? May you find encouragement in the presence of God today and in the promises of his Word.

There is no conflict that Christ has not already won with his love. There are no barriers between us and his flood of mercy. There is more than enough grace to empower each of us in our lives. There is more than enough goodness still being sown into the fabric of the world around us. Let's return to our stronghold, our foundation, and our mighty deliverer. There is restoration on its way.

☐ *Act of Courage*

Dare to believe God will do what he has said he will do and that his presence is enough in the waiting!

Relief in Belief

"Let not your heart be troubled;
you believe in God, believe also in Me."

JOHN 14:1 NKJV

Do you have anyone in your life whom you can truly rely on? Perhaps it is a parent, a friend, or a relative. When they show up, everything feels a little better. When they're around, you can relax because even if what you face is hard, you have someone to help you through it.

God is the ultimate relief for our souls. He is our help at all times. The friendship of Christ is better than any other friendship we know. Or to put it another way, your best friend reflects Christ but just a fraction, for Christ is infinitely more trustworthy and good. When you feel overwhelmed today, ask the Lord to settle your heart with his presence and may you know the relief of him showing up for and with you!

☐ Act of Courage

When you feel overwhelmed, ask God to come alongside you and trust you will get through whatever it is together!

Dance of Deliverance

He delivered us from such a deadly peril,
and he will deliver us. On him we have set our hope
that he will deliver us again.

2 CORINTHIANS 1:10 ESV

Trusting God is not a one-time action. It requires our continual surrender and faith whenever a new challenge arises. Change is inevitable. We will not remain in comfort for the extent of our lives. We will face many challenges and it is important to recognize this, so we are not discouraged when they come. We have not failed when troubles come knocking on our door. It is yet another opportunity for God to deliver us.

When Jesus taught his disciples to pray, one of the tenets he set forth was to ask for the Father to rescue them every time they faced tribulation and he would deliver them from evil (Matthew 6:13). Their prayer is now our prayer. Let us set our hope in Christ, and let's trust him to deliver us time and again before we stand before him in the fullness of his glory!

❏ Act of Courage

*Pray the Lord's Prayer today any time
you begin to feel worried or overwhelmed.*

Under Pressure

If you faint when under pressure,
you have need of courage.

PROVERBS 24:10 TPT

Though our weakness can become an excuse to quit, strength and courage are built as a result of remaining faithful under pressure. How often do we allow something truly difficult to mean we should just give up? Let's not take the easy way out when what we are faced with challenging matters.

The great news for each of us is that we have the Spirit of God to help strengthen us in our weaknesses. He offers us grace when we need it most. Let's not neglect asking for help when the pressures of life get to be too much. Let's build our tolerance for the stretching that comes with discomfort and remain faithful in integrity to what we have been called to do. Let's not give up, for if we don't, we will receive our breakthrough!

☐ *Act of Courage*

When something feels hard today, choose to remain faithful in endurance, asking for help if you need to. Just don't give up!

Always Ready

Preach the Good News. Be ready at all times, and tell people what they need to do. Tell them when they are wrong. Encourage them with great patience and careful teaching.

2 TIMOTHY 4:2 NCV

What does "being ready at all times" really mean? Is it not to meet whatever comes whether it is convenient or not, and to tell the truth with integrity at all times? It takes courage to be honest and faithful when it is inconvenient to do so. It takes strong character to follow through when the odds are stacked against you.

May you stand upon the Word of God as your foundation just as Paul instructs Timothy to do. May you know the peace that passes all understanding as you use wisdom to speak, interact, and serve. May you know the invaluable grace that carries you from moment to moment. There is more than enough for all you need and for whatever you face in the great storehouses of your God. Rely on him above all else, and you will always have what you need at just the right time.

☐ *Act of Courage*

Choose to do the right thing even when it feels inconvenient or unnecessary.

New Things

"Behold, the former things have come to pass,
Now I declare new things;
Before they sprout I proclaim them to you."

ISAIAH 42:9 NASB

In the changing seasons, we catch glimpses of the old things passing away. We create space in the simplicity of winter to let go of what we need to clear away in our lives as we prepare for the barren months. We anticipate new life come spring. The rhythms of nature are cyclical, as are the rhythms of our lives.

We do not stay in endless summer with long days in the sun and bounty surrounding us, nor do we dwell forever in a never-ending winter. May we garner hope from the changes of the seasons, remembering God's Word and his promises as we do so. Even before new life sprouts, God gives us glimpses of it. He shares with us ever so graciously, the hope we need in the waiting.

☐ Act of Courage

Ask God for a glimpse of what is to come while you recognize what season of life you are in at the moment.

Dare to Hope

I still dare to hope when I remember this: The faithful
love of the LORD never ends! His mercies never cease.

LAMENTATIONS 3:21-22 NLT

I think it's `important to recognize what the writer of these
verses was saying directly before this declaration. It was,
in fact, a long lament that ended with, "I will never forget
this awful time, as I grieve over my loss" (3:20). Have you
ever felt that way, being filled with the bitterness of your
suffering and pain?

Yet this is not where the writer leaves his sentiments. It
is reminiscent of the psalmist's declaration: "and yet I will
praise the Lord." Even through the suffering and pain, we
can still dare to hope when we remember that the faithful
love of the Lord never, ever ends! His mercies are new
every morning! Let's take hope and courage from this
truth. Wherever we are, the Lord covers us with new mercy.
We cannot escape the overflow of his loving-kindness from
pouring over us.

☐ Act of Courage

*When you are discouraged, dare to end your lament with,
"Yet, I still dare to hope."*

March

Wait for the LORD;
Be strong and let your heart take courage;
Yes, wait for the LORD.

PSALM 27:14 NASB

Even If

Shadrach, Meshach, and Abed-nego answered and said to the king, "O Nebuchadnezzar, we have no need to answer you in this matter. If that is the case, our God whom we serve is able to deliver us from the burning fiery furnace...But if not, let it be known to you, O king, that we do not serve your gods, nor will we worship the gold image which you have set up."

DANIEL 3:16-18 NKJV

The faith of these three men is a great example for us today. They fully believed God could deliver them from the fiery furnace into which the king was about to throw them. And yet they still left room for the "what if" of God allowing their deaths if he chose to do so. Even if God did not deliver them from the hand of Nebuchadnezzar, they still would not budge on their stance of never worshiping anyone or anything other than Yahweh.

Let's lead with faith and believe God will deliver us! We know the story. The men were thrown into the furnace, but they were not burned. In fact, there was another figure seen with them in the flames. God is with us in the fire.

☐ *Act of Courage*

Choose integrity over compromise even when under threat from others.

Yours to Do

"As for you, be strong; don't give up,
for your work has a reward."

2 Chronicles 15:7 csb

Consistency and follow-through are not the most exciting of attributes, but they help us to persevere through the mundane and the hard times. We can have all the good intentions in the world, but if we lack the courage and tenacity to keep doing the work that is ours to do, we won't get the results we hope for.

It takes strength to endure and to keep going when we are in the messy or boring middle of a task. If we refuse to give up, we will experience our reward. Galatians 6:9 puts it this way, "Let us not grow weary in doing what is right, for we will reap at harvest time, if we do not give up." Wishful thinking will not make changes in our lives, but our consistent work certainly has the potential to do just that. Let's be brave enough to keep our eyes focused on what our work is and do it well!

☐ *Act of Courage*

*Resist the urge to procrastinate and persist in
doing what you know needs to be done.*

Call on Him

The LORD is near to all who call on him,
to all who call on him in truth.

PSALM 145:18 NIV

No matter where you are, no matter what kind of trouble you are facing, God is as close as a whisper. Don't hesitate to bring all your burdens to him. Remember, he sees your heart. He rushes to meet you whenever you call on him.

There is no shame in his presence. He will never use your past against you. He may correct you, but it's always with kindness. He may reprove you, but even so he has undeterred affection for you. A good father corrects his children so they will grow in wisdom, not so he can prove his power. God is a better Father than any of us have known. His love knows no limits, and he will never turn us away when we call on him.

☐ *Act of Courage*

Dare to bring God all that you are—the good, the bad, and the ugly. He receives you with open arms.

A Father's Help

No matter where I am, even when I'm far from home,
I will cry out to you for a father's help.
When I'm feeble and overwhelmed by life,
guide me into your glory, where I am safe and sheltered.

PSALM 61:2 TPT

How can we not feel courage rise within our bones when we know God, the Creator, helps us as a father helps his children whenever we cry out to him? When we are weak and overwhelmed by life, we have a resting place in the presence of God. He is our safe place and our shelter, and he covers us with his care.

No matter where you find yourself today, even if you are as far from home as you have ever been, cry out to God for a father's help. Even if all you need is some advice or to know you are not alone, don't hesitate to call out to him. You are not meant to struggle through on your own. Lean on him and ask him to strengthen you in his presence.

☐ Act of Courage

Ask God for his help and trust he will give it.

Lean In

Be strong in the Lord
and in the strength of his might.

EPHESIANS 6:10 ESV

This statement comes at the end of Paul's letter to the Ephesians. When you've done the good you ought to out of love, when you've done all else, stand "strong in the Lord and in the strength of his might." What a good reminder it is that you don't have to be strong in yourself. You don't have to trust your own abilities at the end of the day. You get to lean into the power of the Lord and to stand in his strength, which he readily shares with you.

Second Corinthians 12:9 says, "My grace is sufficient for you, for my power is made perfect in weakness." No matter how ill-equipped you feel today to face what is ahead of you, know that God's grace is more than enough to empower you in his strength. Lean in and trust him.

Every time you feel weak today,
ask for more grace to persevere in God's strength.

Let Love Lead

Dear friends, we should love each other, because love
comes from God. Everyone who loves has become
God's child and knows God. Whoever does not love
does not know God, because God is love.

1 JOHN 4:7-8 NCV

Jesus' teachings are not suggestions. They are the very
heart of God. We cannot claim to know God and yet refuse
to walk in love. It is a contradiction in terms. God is love.
Full stop; no exceptions. He is the source of love. He leaves
no excuse for us to cling to in withholding love from others.
Let's remember that love is kind though it is not always
easy to choose. It is not fluffy or disingenuous. It is not a
superficial niceness. It is a merciful motivation that drives
us to choose to err on the side of justice, to side with
the vulnerable instead of the powerful, and to act out of
compassion rather than self-protection.

May we grow in love, removing the barriers that systems
and people and even ourselves have put upon it. The love
of God is limitless, so let's expand our own!

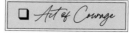

*Choose to act with love today when you would rather
dismiss another who would be blessed by your grace.*

Courage to Rejoice

Give thanks to the LORD, for he is good!
His faithful love endures forever.

1 CHRONICLES 16:34 NLT

Sometimes praise comes easily, and sometimes it is a choice. When we struggle to see the goodness of God beyond the struggles of life, it is an act of courage to give thanks to the Lord. His nature is unchanging. He is always full of unfailing mercy. He is always good, even when we cannot understand his ways.

The Word tells us that the steadfast love of God never ends, and his mercies never cease (Lamentations 3:22). There is fresh mercy every morning, every moment, in fact. There is more than enough help in the presence of our Good Father to face whatever comes. Let's turn our attention to his unchanging mercy, his indescribable goodness, and his faithfulness. "Though I am surrounded by troubles...you reach out your hand, and the power of your right hand saves me" (Psalm 138:7). Whether in times of comfort or conflict, the Lord remains the same in love.

❑ *Act of Courage*

When you struggle to turn your attention to praise, read Psalm 138.

Courage to Believe

Only goodness and faithful love will pursue me all the days of my life, and I will dwell in the house of the Lord as long as I live.

PSALM 23:6 CSB

Earlier in this renowned psalm, David asserts, "Even though I walk through the darkest valley, I fear no evil; for you are with me; your rod and your staff—they comfort me." The Lord is a Good Shepherd, guiding us through the valleys and pitfalls of this life. Even as he directs us through the darkest nights, his presence is our promised comfort and peace.

Do you believe God is with you? Do you believe he is for you? His love compels him in everything he does. He is full of mercy, justice, and truth. He does not lie, manipulate, or ridicule. He is better than the best of humanity. May you have the courage to believe that his goodness and mercy follows you, for his presence sows the seeds of his kingdom.

☐ Act of Courage

Whenever you feel overwhelmed by life today, remember this verse and speak it over yourself.

Stepping Out

Lord, look at their threats, and grant it to Your bond-servants to speak Your word with all confidence, while You extend Your hand to heal, and signs and wonders take place through the name of Your holy servant Jesus.

ACTS 4:29-30 NASB

When faced with threats from others, what is your reaction? Is it to fight back and return the bitterness, or is it to call out to God? Notice here, the prayer is not for others to experience retaliation but the breakthrough of God's Spirit in their midst. It is for the strength to speak the truth with confidence, and to be vessels of the miraculous movement of the Spirit.

May you be filled with the Holy Spirit just as the believers were who prayed this prayer. May you know the overwhelming boldness which comes through the empowering presence of God with and in you. May you experience the indescribable goodness of his power moving through you as you partner with his purposes. May you experience breakthrough and be a vessel of breakthrough for others!

❏ *Act of Courage*

Pray for confidence and for the infilling power of the Spirit today.

Marvelous Mercy

The LORD our God is merciful and forgiving,
even though we have rebelled against him.

DANIEL 9:9 NIV

Even when we rebel against God by doing what we know
we shouldn't, God is still merciful and forgiving. He does
not abandon us even when wander off on our own. He
is better than that. His love never wavers, not even for a
second. He is as full of loyal love today as he was when
you first came to him. He is more wonderful than you
can imagine, so increase your expectations to meet the
expanse of his goodness!

What wonderful courage and confidence we have in
the gloriously unchanging mercy of Christ! Though we
fail, often and hard, sometimes, he does not. Though we
think we know better, his wisdom is patient. Every time
we experience his forgiveness, we grow in the marvelous
mercy he offers us. May our perspectives expand in his
great and gracious love. May we have more courage to
live in his love every time we experience new degrees of it
ourselves!

☐ *Act of Courage*

*Return to the Lord today and receive
his faithful forgiveness.*

Ready Wisdom

The wisdom that comes from God is first of all pure, then peaceful, gentle, and easy to please. This wisdom is always ready to help those who are troubled and to do good for others. It is always fair and honest.

JAMES 3:17 NCV

Wisdom does not rub others' noses in its greatness. It is pure, peaceful, gentle, and humble. It is ready to help those in need and to do good for others. It is honest and fair, just and kind. It is easy to please. As with many of the teachings of Christ, it is subversive to the mainstream culture, and even the religious systems. When we lean into the wisdom of Christ, we don't have to worry about what others will say, for the favor of God is better than the favor of humanity.

As we make decisions, may we do so with the kind of wisdom that comes from God. May we rely on the ways of Christ to direct us and not popular opinion. There is integrity in the wisdom of God. It takes courage to walk in the laid-down-love of Christ, putting his kingdom above our own interests. May we be brave enough to follow him in the little and the big things.

❑ *Act of Courage*

Weigh your decisions with the wisdom of Christ as outlined in this verse.

Strength to Strength

Blessed is the man whose strength is in You,
Whose heart is set on pilgrimage.
As they pass through the Valley of Baca,
They make it a spring;
The rain also covers it with pools.
They go from strength to strength;
Each one appears before God in Zion.

PSALM 84:5-7 NKJV

The Valley of Baca can be translated as "the dark valley of tears." When the lovers of God walk through times of deep suffering and grief, they dig deep to find a pleasant pool where others only find pain. There is a brook of blessing for those who press into the presence of God. There is more blessing than we can imagine. Even in the hardest times of our lives, we are never without him.

May we grow stronger with every step forward, going from strength to strength with the help of the Holy Spirit. When we don't give up but keep living and moving, the grace of God goes with us. May we always seek the presence of God which is already with us, turning our attention to his nearness.

❑ Act of Courage

Press on when things feel hard today, and more than anything, press into the presence of God.

Perspective Shifts

You, O LORD, are a shield about me,
my glory, and the lifter of my head.

PSALM 3:3 ESV

God, the head-lifter and perspective-shifter, is the one who breathes hope into our weary souls. He is the God who breathes on dry bones and brings them to life. He is the one who redeems our broken dreams and brings new opportunities out of the ashes of our defeat. He is never at a loss for what to do, and he always has a plan of redemption and restoration when we only see death and destruction.

Instead of giving in to the despair of a cruel world, let's allow the Lord to lift our heads to meet his eyes. In his eyes we will find the love, the grace, and the courage to rise again. Through his perspective we are able to see what we could not understand on our own. His view is greater than our own, and he doesn't miss a thing.

☐ *Act of Courage*

Ask God to lift your head when you feel hopeless.

Forgive Again

Make allowance for each other's faults, and forgive anyone who offends you. Remember, the Lord forgave you, so you must forgive others.

COLOSSIANS 3:13 NLT

When Peter asked Jesus how many times he would have to forgive his fellow believer who kept offending him, Jesus' response was much more than a number: "Not seven times, Peter, but seventy times seven" (Matthew 18). He was illustrating a point; we must be willing to forgive others countless times more than we would ever choose. Why? Because that is what his love does for us.

We cannot quantify God's mercy. It is limitless. So, when we venture to live in it, we must remove the boundaries of worldly common sense. As often as we are offended, that is how many times we can forgive. When we make allowances for each other's faults, we recognize the humanity in each other. Let's stop putting limits on mercy because Christ never does!

☐ *Act of Courage*

Choose to forgive—again and again!— the offenses of others against you.

Endless Hope

"Keep your hope to the end
and you will experience life and deliverance."

MATTHEW 24:13 TPT

Jesus just finished giving a pretty dour prediction of what
would happen to his disciples in the verses before our
verse for today. He explained how they would suffer in
various ways. And yet he said, "but keep your hope to the
end." In the next verse Jesus continued, "Yet through it all,
this joyful assurance of the realm of heaven's kingdom will
be proclaimed all over the world, providing every nation
with a demonstration of the reality of God."

This is our promised reality, here and now. The glimpse of
God's heaven touching earth, and "providing every nation
with...the reality of God." Even though we suffer in this
life in a variety of ways, we have a joyful assurance in the
realm of God's kingdom! Let's hold on to hope, just as the
originator of our hope holds on to us.

*Even in the face of pain choose to hold on to hope,
for it is not the end.*

Good Plans

"For I know the plans I have for you"—this is the LORD's declaration—"plans for your well-being, not for disaster, to give you a future and a hope."

JEREMIAH 29:11 CSB

Not all that happens in our lives is a result of our choices. Some things happen *to* us. It is in these tough places where we must garner courage. God is a God of redemption. He can bring life from even the most destitute of places. There is never a situation he cannot lead us out of with his love. We are never without his mercy. We are never without hope.

Even when we don't understand *why* things are happening the way they are, here's some brutal and beautiful news: we don't have to make everything in life a lesson or to make sense of all things. We can trust the victorious one who will make all things right. Let's have the courage to trust the power of his love, and that he will lead us into his goodness.

□ *Act of Courage*

Trust that if you are in the midst of suffering, this is not the end of your story.

Don't Give Up

We must not become tired of doing good.
We will receive our harvest of eternal life
at the right time if we do not give up.

GALATIANS 6:9 NCV

It takes courage to keep choosing to do the right thing when others are looking for ways to bypass the work involved. In a world that values efficiency over integrity, choosing the latter way requires willpower. We don't choose God's ways simply because he tells us to. There is so much wisdom and promise in making Christ's kingdom values our own.

Whenever we have the opportunity, let's do good, not only to those we like but to everyone. We reflect the heart of God when we love each other the way Christ loves us. "All people will know that you are my followers if you love each other," Jesus said in John 13:35. Let's take courage in his promise: "I give them eternal life, and they will never die, and no one can steal them out of my hand" (John 10:28). The giver of life offers us eternity in his kingdom, so let's not give up following his ways here and now!

☐ Act of Courage

*Do good to everyone you are around today,
every chance you get!*

Known and Loved

"You who are treasured, do not be afraid. Peace be to you; take courage and be courageous!" Now as soon as he spoke to me, I felt strengthened and said, "May my lord speak, for you have strengthened me."

DANIEL 10:19 NASB

We all long to be seen and known by others in our lives. We long for relationships that validate our worth as well as our potential. When someone says to us, "I see you, I value you, and I love you," does that not bring a balm of peace to our hearts? From the unshakeable foundation of strong relationships, we can take courage and strength!

Who in your life infuses you with courage when you talk to them? Whose presence brings a settled peace to your heart? These are gifts of God, and they are glimpses of the Lord's great love and fiery faithfulness for you. May you feel strengthened by the words of those who see, know, love, and encourage you.

☐ *Act of Courage*

Reach out to a friend and encourage them by sharing how much they mean to you.

Complete Trust

Trust in the Lord completely,
and do not rely on your own opinions.
With all your heart rely on him to guide you,
and he will lead you in every decision you make.
Become intimate with him in whatever you do,
and he will lead you wherever you go.
Don't think for a moment that you know it all.

PROVERBS 3:5-6 TPT

Total trust in the Lord means you trust him more than
you do your own opinions. Relying on him to lead you in
every decision means you can confidently walk into the
future. Even as paths are being cleared in the wilderness,
he makes a way for you where you could see none. He is
faithful to guide you, and you will have the rest which his
peaceful presence brings.

Whatever your level of trust is today, nurture the relationship
you have with him. Give him your time and attention asking
him to reveal more of himself to you. Invite his Spirit to shift
your perspective as he reveals the wisdom of the Father.
Whatever you do, invite him into it. Remain teachable in his
love and follow him. As you do, your trust will grow.

☐ Act of Courage

*Choose to trust the Lord more than you
trust your own opinions today.*

Feed Yourself

They all were encouraged
and ate some food themselves.

ACTS 27:36 ESV

When we are overwhelmed with worry, we can forget to do the things we normally take for granted. In fact, it may feel almost impossible to continue on with the mundane aspects of life when tragedy strikes. Yet if we neglect ourselves, we will waste away. Sometimes we need to follow the lead of others who break bread, thank God for it, and then eat. Sometimes the best thing to do is to feed our bodies.

Is there an area of your being that you have been neglecting? Perhaps you have not been eating as regularly as your body needs, or you haven't been moving your body enough. Perhaps you have neglected the friendships in your life in favor of getting ahead at work. Take some time to really evaluate the areas that need your attention and have the courage to meet your needs today.

☐ Act of Courage

It is an act of courage to reject neglect and treat yourself with dignity. Feed yourself whatever you need today.

Return and Wait

You must return to your God;
maintain love and justice,
and wait for your God always.

HOSEA 12:6 NIV

In an age of instant access and gratification, it has become a challenge to wait. God does not move in our time frame, and he often uses the process of waiting to refine us and make us ready. Let's take courage from the words of Peter: "With the Lord a day is like a thousand years, and a thousand years are like a day. The Lord is not slow in keeping his promise... instead he is patient with you" (2 Peter 3:8-9).

The Lord is patient, so let's practice some of that patience ourselves. Let's return to our God, keeping love at the forefront, and pursuing justice. Let's wait for our God no matter how long it takes. Instead of rushing ahead with fear as our motivation, let's wait on God and allow his peace to fill us.

Act of Courage

Instead of reacting in the heat of the moment as so many others do, take time and wait before you respond.

Rescue Mission

Rescue those who are being taken away to death,
And those who are staggering to the slaughter,
Oh hold them back!

PROVERBS 24:11 NASB

This proverb continues by cutting out the argument before we can even utter it. God sees through our excuses, and he will hold us responsible when we fail to help others. Let's not stay unwilling to get scarred or dirty but make the business of those who are crying out for help our own business. God is not only the keeper of our souls but of all souls!

Let's have the courage to intervene when we see others struggling on death's door. Let's feed the hungry, offer help to those stuck in cycles of oppression, and be the voices of freedom that not only say they care but also fight for their neighbor's liberty as much as our own. God is a God of rescue, and he does not overlook anyone, so let's not allow our vision to be dulled when we're out in the world.

☐ *Act of Courage*

Pay for a stranger's meal today.

Call to Rejoice

My brothers, rejoice in the Lord. To write the same things to you is no trouble to me and is safe for you.

PHILIPPIANS 3:1 ESV

In another translation, this verse reads, "Don't ever limit your joy or fail to rejoice in the wonderful experience of knowing our Lord Jesus!" (TPT). When it all comes down to it, rejoice in the Lord. When you are sick, rejoice in him. When you are well, rejoice in him. When you are on top of the world, rejoice. When you are disappointed, still rejoice. At all times, in all ways, we have access to our great Savior and loving Father through his Spirit. If for no other reason, that is a reason to rejoice!

Have you ever looked for a way to reframe your experience in the light of God's love? It does not mean you have to deny the hard realities. You can be suffering and still see where God's mercy meets you. You can be grieving and still recognize God's comfort is near. May you find courage to rejoice in the Lord today no matter where you are or what you are dealing with.

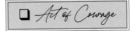

□ *Act of Courage*

When you are discouraged, offended, sad, mad—you name it!—make it a practice to add, "And still I rejoice in you, Lord!"

Prevailing Peace

Since we have been justified through faith, we have peace with God through our Lord Jesus Christ.

ROMANS 5:1 NIV

Peace is a promise from Jesus to us. "Peace I leave with you; my peace I give you." These are Jesus' words in John 14 to his disciples. The peace God offers us through faith is not weak, and it is not temporary. It is a permanent, prevailing peace!

Even when we are overwhelmed, the peace of God is close. Let's find our rest in the presence of his Spirit, and let's turn our attention to the comfort he offers. If it is true that we are at peace with God, then we can courageously face whatever comes. He does not condemn us, so why would we condemn ourselves? He does not keep us tethered by fear, so why would we let fear direct our decisions? Let's follow the leading of his peace, and let's rise up and keep pressing on in bold confidence.

☐ *Act of Courage*

Rest in the peace God has offered you.
Let your heart soak in the knowledge
that his love covers you.

Righteous Pursuits

Flee from youthful lusts and pursue righteousness, faith, love, and peace with those who call on the Lord from a pure heart.

2 TIMOTHY 2:22 NASB

Life is about so much more than superficial pursuits. What are the things that last a lifetime? May we focus on these things, turning aside from passing desires and ambitions that will not lead us to where we long to be. Let's have the courage to pursue what nourishes our purity, builds our faith, and deepens our love. Against these things there is no law. Galatians 5:22-23 instructs us in the fruit of the Spirit. When we aren't sure what we should pursue, let's use these attributes as a measuring stick. Does our decision reflect the fruit of the Spirit, leading us into peace, or does it lead us away from it?

As we chase after all that is found in the kingdom of Christ, our lives transform in the overwhelming mercy of God. What once seemed impossible becomes possible. What once felt distant comes close. What pursuits can you trade today?

□ *Act of Courage*

Ask the Lord for clarity to know what to focus on and work toward.

Clothed in Love

Love is patient and kind. Love is not jealous,
it does not brag, and it is not proud.

1 CORINTHIANS 13:4 NCV

When we are mistreated, it can be easy to convince
ourselves that we can throw love out the window. Yet
that is not what Christ calls us to do. His kingdom, his
teachings, and his life are incredibly countercultural and,
in some cases, opposite to our human nature. Where we
would strike those who attack us, Jesus calls us to a better
way. His instruction to turn the other cheek is not a nice
sentiment; it is a powerful act of surrendered love.

It takes courage to choose this kind of love. It takes
an incredible amount of trust to walk in patience and
kindness, offering compassion instead of hatred. When we
walk the path of Christ's love, we choose his kingdom's
principles over our own. His love is beautiful. He is patient,
kind, generous, and wonderful to us. May we offer the
same kind of love to others!

☐ *Act of Courage*

*Choose patience and kindness in your interactions
with people, even the frustrating ones!*

Securely Fastened

> "Whoever listens to me will live securely
> and be undisturbed by the dread of danger."
>
> PROVERBS 1:33 CSB

When we align our lives in the wisdom of Christ, we choose the path of his everlasting life rather than the destruction that comes from following foolish whims. When we embrace wise correction and counsel, we expand in understanding. When we ignore it, we eat the bitter fruit of our own mistakes.

With wisdom as our guide, we are free from fear. We can be confident and courageous, resting unafraid of the storms of life. Perhaps we can take a cue from Jesus, who, in the midst of a fierce storm, slept through it. His perfect peace becomes our own as he shares his powerful presence with us. May we know how firmly connected we are to his peace, choosing to walk in the ways of his wisdom all the days of our lives. It is so very worth it!

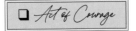

❏ *Act of Courage*

Choose to listen to and apply the wisdom of Christ to your decisions today, even (and especially) if it's hard!

Power at Work

"As soon as we heard it, our hearts melted with fear, and we were left with no courage among us because of you. Yahweh, your God, is the true God who rules in heaven above and on earth below."

JOSHUA 2:11 TPT

When God is on our side, we have nothing to fear. And yet, if we reject to live out his love in our lives, we may find ourselves echoing what the people said in response to God's power on behalf of the Israelites.

As we embrace the ways of Christ's kingdom, surrendering ourselves to his leadership and love, we can take courage in knowing that God, the true God who rules over all, is dependable. He is reliable in mercy, and he is overwhelmingly sufficient in power. Let's lean on his strength in our weakness, trusting him to do what he said he would. He is faithful!

☐ *Act of Courage*

Surrender to God's leadership and trust him to do what he said he will do.

Faithful Friends

Jonathan went to find David and encouraged him to
stay strong in his faith in God.

1 SAMUEL 23:16 NLT

Have you ever gone down a deep, dark discouraging spiral
when you're alone? Even the strongest among us are
human. No one is immune to pain, suffering, or despair. It is
not a failure to be weak, though many of us may struggle
with this. There's a reason we are not meant to go it
alone in life, and one of those reasons is that we need the
encouragement, strength, comfort, and hope of others.

When we see others struggling, may we come alongside
them and encourage them to keep going. When we
ourselves are struggling, may we have the courage to
reach out to trusted friends with the reality of our pain.
Let's be brave enough to be vulnerable and to let others
see our vulnerability. When others witness and encourage
us in that place, it can be like a balm soothing our fears
and strengthening our souls.

☐ Act of Courage

*Reach out to a friend. Go to their house, send them a note,
or buy them some flowers. Encourage them to keep going.*

Diligent Peace

Beloved, looking forward to these things, be diligent to be found by Him in peace, without spot and blameless.

2 PETER 3:14 NKJV

Why does Peter say to "be diligent to be found by Him [Christ] in peace"? Could it be because it is more natural for us to worry than it is to trust in a world filled with uncertainty? May we fix our eyes on the unchanging One, reminding our hearts of his goodness and faithfulness as often as we think of it today.

May peace be our persistent portion as we become diligent in turning our attention to Christ with us. He never leaves us, and he won't begin now. We can trust his presence, his love, and his comfort. Even when the earth shakes, he remains unmoved. His character is steadfast, and his peace is always available. Think of a cue you can use to turn your attention to his peace, whether it is birdsong, a piece of jewelry , or a habit that you consistently do. Every time you notice the cue, remind yourself of his peace which permeates the space you inhabit.

☐ Act of Courage

Use a physical cue to remind yourself of receiving the peace of God over and over again.

Wholehearted Search

If from there you seek the LORD your God,
you will find him if you seek him
with all your heart and with all your soul.

DEUTERONOMY 4:29 NIV

Jesus promised, "Ask and it will be given to you; seek and you will find; knock and the door will be opened to you" (Matthew 7:7). Every persistent searcher will discover what they long for, including you. This is a principle of the kingdom of Christ.

What is it you spend your time, energy, and attention searching for? Is it satisfying? There is really good news in the gospel of Christ. No matter how much time we feel we have wasted, when we turn ourselves in reorientation and redirection, God meets us in it. No matter what you have been searching for, if you seek God with all of your heart and soul, you will find him. So, keep going. Keep searching. Have courage and look for where his light breaks through!

☐ Act of Courage

Choose to seek God's perspective today over your life and ask for him to reveal himself to you in new ways.

April

The wicked run away
when no one is chasing them,
but the godly are as bold as lions.

PROVERBS 28:1 NLT

Comfort to Share

*If we are afflicted, it is for your comfort and salvation;
and if we are comforted, it is for your comfort, which
you experience when you patiently endure the same
sufferings that we suffer.*

2 CORINTHIANS 1:6 ESV

What we receive, we are able to pass along to others.
That is the gist of what Paul is saying here. Even in our
suffering, we are not bereft; we receive comfort. If we have
experienced comfort, then we also have comfort to offer
others. We don't have to have it all together, whatever that
means, in order to help others. Even in the midst of our
pain and our troubles, we are not without the help of the
Holy Spirit. If we have the Holy Spirit, then we always have
something to offer.

May you take courage in whatever you are facing today.
May you not feel forgotten or overlooked. May you know
the nearness and comfort of the Spirit of God who holds
you close. May you take encouragement in knowing
whatever you receive you also can give to others.

☐ *Act of Courage*

*Look at what you have received recently
and find ways to offer that to others today.*

Confession and Prayer

Confess your sins to one another, and pray for one another so that you may be healed. A prayer of a righteous person, when it is brought about, can accomplish much.

JAMES 5:16 NASB

It takes courage to admit where we have gone wrong. It is no easy or small task to confront the ways we fail others, God, and ourselves. When we confess our failures to others and humble our hearts before them, we are given the opportunity to connect on a deeper level. The same is true for when we humble ourselves before God and ask for forgiveness and the strength to change.

Prayer is an act of recognizing we cannot rely upon ourselves or our own strength. When we pray for others, we are offering them our care as well as opening our hearts to compassion. May we have courage to both confess and be hearers of confession, demonstrating humility on both ends. There is power in being seen, power in telling the truth, and power in prayer.

☐ *Act of Courage*

Have a vulnerable and real conversation with a trusted friend today and pray together.

Mindful of Others

LORD, why are people important to you?
Why do you even think about human beings?
People are like a breath; their lives are like
passing shadows.

PSALM 144:3-4 NCV

Our lives on this earth are but short stints in the scope of eternity. Yet God is mindful of each one of us. He created us in love, and he is concerned about us. It is almost too much to know the God who knows no limits, boundaries, or power but is mindful of me and you! And yet it is true.

Are we also mindful of others around us? May we see from a bigger scope and not just the small lens of our little lives. May we have the courage to truly see others, knowing that connection is what we were created for. Just as God thinks of you, he thinks of those you fail to even notice. May his compassion expand your worldview and allow you to see those whom he never misses. Maybe, just maybe, you will find an aspect of God's love you didn't know was even possible in the face of one who reflects his image uniquely.

Act of Courage

*Make it a priority to intentionally notice
the people you are around today.*

Nothing Compares

I once thought these things were valuable,
but now I consider them worthless
because of what Christ has done.

PHILIPPIANS 3:7 NLT

There is nothing wrong with reaching for achievement.
However, when it becomes synonymous with our worth, we
have some reevaluating to do. Have you ever experienced
the fulfillment of a long-held dream and then realized
the feeling of satisfaction was fleeting? Even momentous
accomplishments lose their luster as days pass.

Instead of being discouraged by this reality, let's adjust our
focus. We don't need to forsake our lives, our loved ones,
or what we've worked for in order to have a mindset shift
to the perspective held by Christ. As we are transformed
by the incomparable mercy of Jesus, we may feel led to
change course. We don't have to try to figure out what he
will lead us into. Let's trust him and turn our hearts to him.
Nothing compares to the lasting love, peace, joy, and hope
of Christ's restoration in our souls to the Father's heart.
Through him, we find satisfaction that does not waver.

☐ *Act of Courage*

*Give your heart to truly knowing Christ
and his perspective of your life.*

Wonderful Understanding

"Blessed are your eyes for they see,
and your ears for they hear."

MATTHEW 13:16 NKJV

In the Spirit of Christ, we have access to the same miracles Jesus performed in the years of his ministry. Through faith, we receive. In his name, we experience freedom, love, peace, and joy. Let's not neglect the invitation of Christ to walk in his ways and experience the power of his Spirit!

Jesus told his disciples that those who follow him will do the same mighty miracles he did (John 14:12). In fact, he said they would do even greater things. May our eyes see and our ears hear what the Spirit is actively doing and saying as we partner with the purposes of Christ in welcoming his kingdom to earth through our surrendered lives! There is much more than we have yet experienced available to us. Let's continue to press into his presence and yield to his leadership in our lives.

☐ Act of Courage

Ask the Holy Spirit to move through you in mighty ways and walk in obedience to his leadership!

Courage in Kindness

Act wisely toward outsiders, making the most of the
time. Let your speech always be gracious, seasoned
with salt, so that you may know how you should answer
each person.

COLOSSIANS 4:5-6 CSB

The ways of the kingdom of Christ do not only apply to the
way we treat other believers. Kindness should be shown
to everyone. We should be clothed in his mercy in every
interaction and relationship. No one is left out of the love
of God, so let's resist the urge to meter it out ourselves.
Let's have the courage to be kind, even to those who show
no kindness to us.

Love is not love when it finds reasons to withhold itself
from those whom it doesn't get along. Love is patient,
kind, and gentle. It is not jealous, and it doesn't rub others'
noses in its successes. Reflect the overwhelmingly good
and abundant love of Christ. Fill up on his mercy and
kindness in the morning, spend all you have, and refill at
the end of the day. Choose the harder path of love, and
reject pettiness, judgment, and revenge.

❑ Act of Courage

*Read through 1 Corinthians 13 and let it challenge the way
you interact with others today!*

Lifestyle of Prayer

All day long God's promises of love pour over me.
Through the night I sing his songs,
for my prayer to God has become my life.

PSALM 42:8 TPT

There is not a moment when God's promises of love are not pouring over you. Think about that. Soak it in! Right now, he is lavishing the love song of his affection over your life and over your very being!

God's love is not just to be known about. It is to be experienced. No matter how long or little it's been since you've felt the love of the Lord, may you be drenched in the goodness of his heart toward you today. Right now, even as you read these words, may the Spirit of God flood you with the light of his mercy. Let your heart open in response, and let your lifestyle be a living prayer to the God who calls you his own!

❏ *Act of Courage*

Ask the Lord to reveal his presence to you in deep, tangible ways. Offer him your heartfelt praise in response.

No Need to Fear

"Do not fear, for I am with you;
do not be dismayed, for I am your God.
I will strengthen you and help you;
I will uphold you with my righteous right hand."

ISAIAH 41:10 NIV

How confident are you that God is there to help you? He won't just help you if you live a picture-perfect lifestyle or appear righteous to others. He helps you every time you cry out to him. He is as close to the utterly defeated as he is to any other. Don't hesitate to call out to him. He will strengthen you and help you, no questions asked.

What we receive from God, we often don't even know to ask for. Let's lean on his presence, and let's trust his wisdom to give us all we need with the power of his grace. Let's have the courage to trust him, even when our hearts are rippling. His steady grip of grace is on our lives. He is near, and he won't let go!

☐ Act of Courage

Walk out what God has put before you today and trust him to help you with whatever you need along the way. He is with you.

Solid Foundation

Let your roots grow down into him,
and let your lives be built on him.
Then your faith will grow strong
in the truth you were taught,
and you will overflow with thankfulness.

COLOSSIANS 2:7 NLT

What would it look like for you to build your life upon the foundation of Christ? What could you do to set your house in order, so to speak? His wisdom is helpful for all kinds of situations. His strength is even more palpable in the weakness of humanity.

Give yourself permission to grow in him imperfectly, and to take the next step without knowing what the end product will be. There are a hundred steps between planning something and the fulfillment of that thing. Have the courage to not get ahead of yourself, but to trust as you grow strong in the truth of Christ, that your faith will grow, and his grace will empower you every step of the way.

☐ Act of Courage

Only do what you know to do today. Give your energy to today's projects and let tomorrow stay where it is – in the future.

Shield of Strength

The LORD is my strength and my shield;
My heart trusts in Him, and I am helped;
Therefore my heart triumphs,
And with my song I shall thank Him.

PSALM 28:7 NASB

The Lord is described many times in the psalms as being a source of protection for his people . Specifically, the term "shield" is often used as an image to evoke the very near strength and security of God. In Psalm 3:3, David says, "You, Lord, are a shield around me, My glory, and the One who lifts my head."

God is our guard and the watchman over our souls. He diffuses the attacks of the enemy, and we can rest in his trustworthy and powerful nature. May our hearts trust him completely, causing us to rejoice in the victory we share with him because of Christ. Even as we experience his triumph in the liberty and protection of our souls, we can know his fullness, no matter where we are!

☐ Act of Courage

Whenever you are tempted to be overcome by fear or worry today, picture the protective love of Christ as a shield completely surrounding you.

Slow Down

My dear brothers and sisters, understand this:
Everyone should be quick to listen,
slow to speak, and slow to anger.

JAMES 1:19 CSB

Everyone loves a good success story. Who doesn't enjoy the tale of an underdog overcoming their circumstances and experiencing breakthrough? In the nitty-gritty of our own lives though, we may feel as if our timeline doesn't match our expectations. Much of what we don't absorb in the stories of others is often the long journey of struggle that it can take to get to where they are.

There is wisdom in slowing down and not moving ahead in haste. When we give space both to ourselves and to others, to really listen, absorb, and understand, it is not a waste of time but a good use of it. May we have the courage to become less reactive and more thoughtful, even as others continue to rush ahead. We will not miss out on anything important by choosing to do this, but we certainly might if we ignore the need to listen with an open heart.

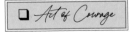

☐ Act of Courage

When you don't understand someone, take time to ask them questions and really listen to where they are coming from.

Whatever Comes

"Behold, God is my salvation, I will trust and not be afraid; 'For YAH, the LORD, is my strength and song; He also has become my salvation.'"

ISAIAH 12:2 NKJV

As we trust God to guide us through this life, we should not expect to bypass pain. It is not possible! As long as we live in this world, we will experience the full spectrum of humanity. There is so much joy to experience, but there is also suffering. There is peace, love, and hope, and there is also disappointment, loss, and grief.

It is not a failure to feel these things. The Spirit is known as the Comforter for a reason. Don't be afraid to recognize the hard aspects of life. Even in these moments you will grow in grace, love, and peace. You will have a deeper understanding of the mercy of Christ if you allow him to meet you in it. Trust, and don't be afraid of what comes. God is your salvation no matter what you walk through! Take his hand and trust him to be with you no matter what.

☐ *Act of Courage*

Let the Lord's persistent presence be your reason for thanks today.

Heard and Answered

I am passionately in love with God
because he listens to me.
He hears my prayers and answers them.

PSALM 116:1 TPT

This beautiful, celebratory psalm continues by saying, "As long as I live, I'll keep praying to him, for he stoops down to listen to my heart's cry...He was so kind, so gracious to me. Because of his passion toward me, he made everything right and he restored me" (verses 2, 5). Have you ever been overwhelmed by relief? This is what the writer of this psalm was expressing.

Perhaps you have known this type of relief, and maybe you are still waiting for your breakthrough. Don't stop hoping in the Lord! What he has done before, he will do again. What he has promised, he will fulfill. He is skilled at restoring that which looks completely decimated in our eyes. He is better than we could ever imagine, so let's put our complete hope in his unfailing love and wait on his kindness.

☐ Act of Courage

Have the courage to keep praying, trusting, and persevering. Your God hears you, and he will answer you!

Prepare Yourself

Take up the whole armor of God, that you may be able
to withstand in the evil day, and having done all,
to stand firm.

EPHESIANS 6:13 ESV

May you take the time to refresh your understanding of
the armor of God today, reading through the sixth chapter
of Ephesians. God provides you with all you need to be
protected as you stand firm in the knowledge of Christ.
You don't have to do anything by figuring it out on your
own. He has offered you everything you need by his Spirit
who lives in you.

Although it is not by your strength alone that you stand,
you can take steps to prepare yourself according to God's
Word. Don't neglect the part you play! Just as you would
not expect others to dress you when you are able to do so
yourself, there are things you can do in preparing yourself
spiritually. With intention, follow-through, and plenty of
grace, you will stand firm on the foundation of Christ's
incomparable mercy.

❑ Act of Courage

*Take ownership of what is yours to do today and
rejoice in the help you receive when you ask for it!*

Reason to Hope

All you who put your hope in the LORD
be strong and brave.

PSALM 31:24 NCV

Why would we reject God's help when it is so ready and
near? Let's lay down our pride, setting aside our self-
sufficiency, and lean into the present empowering grace
of the Spirit of God. No matter what we are dealing with,
the Lord can be trusted to help us, and it is no weak,
small thing! We are not afterthoughts to the Lord. He sees
everything we struggle with, and he cares about even the
smallest details we may dismiss.

God's love is greater than our understanding could ever
fathom. He is infinitely kinder, more powerful, and wiser
than we can perceive. Instead of relying upon our own
limited resources today, let's stand on the foundation of his
faithfulness, and take courage. Let's rise up in the hope of
his wonderful mercy, and let's not let our situations dictate
his goodness!

❏ *Act of Courage*

*Look beyond your circumstances to the unchanging
and indescribably good nature of Christ.
Let that be your courage today!*

Spirit Power

God will never give you the spirit of fear,
but the Holy Spirit who gives you mighty power,
love, and self-control.

2 TIMOTHY 1:7 TPT

If there is any way to decipher what is from God and what is not, let's look at the character and the fruit. We know God does not manipulate, shame, or demean. He does not use his power to threaten others. He does not taunt or tempt us. All he does is in love because *God is love.*

Our perceptions are faulty, but God's power is not. Where we have limited understanding, God is unlimited in wisdom and faithfulness. Instead of trying to figure God out according to our own failures and limitations, let's allow our understanding to expand in his wisdom. We become transformed by his love as he lavishes it over us. His Spirit gives mighty power, mercy, and self-control. What wonderful gifts we have in him!

❑ *Act of Courage*

Allow your mind to be changed as you consider God's great power. It takes courage to reevaluate and transform your thinking!

Note the Details

Go, inspect the city of Jerusalem. Walk around and count the many towers. Take note of the fortified walls, and tour all the citadels, that you may describe them to future generations. For that is what God is like. He is our God forever and ever, and he will guide us until we die.

PSALM 48:12-14 NLT

When God moves in our lives, let's not simply move on to the next thing. Let's look at the details, poring over the glory of his marvelous mercy! Let's record what it is we see, feel, and experience of his glory so we may pass it on to future generations. Let's keep it in a place we can come back to so our hearts may be encouraged by God's loyal love!

God's mercy is as practical as it is mighty. What he sets in place, no one can remove. When is the last time you were encouraged by the testimony of someone experiencing a miracle that could not be explained away by mere chance or logic? There is beauty in mystery, and we should embrace it as we are remembering the tangible goodness of God in our lives.

☐ *Act of Courage*

Think of a time when God moved on your behalf, or in the life of someone you love, and write down every detail about it that you can remember.

Inspired by Encouragement

Both Judas and Silas, who were also prophets
themselves, encouraged the brothers and sisters
and strengthened them with a long message.

Acts 15:32 csb

If you are familiar with Gary Chapman's work about love
languages, you are probably well acquainted with the term,
"words of affirmation." In short, it is giving or receiving
encouraging words about who a person is, what they are
doing right, or helpful reminders of what they mean to others.

For some, affirming and encouraging others comes
naturally. For others, it takes a concerted effort to share. In
any case, encouragement can strengthen us when we are
feeling discouraged, uplift us when we are feeling down,
and bolster our sense of resolve in being our best selves.
Our own sense of peace, joy, and love is reinforced as we
share the goodness we see in others. Let's be unashamed
encouragers!

☐ Act of Courage

*Share specific things you love and appreciate about the
people in your life with them today. Be more generous
with your words than you normally are!*

Compassionate Care

"In the same way your Father in heaven is not willing
that any of these little ones should perish."

MATTHEW 18:14 NIV

Jesus used the parable of a lost lamb to illustrate how
he acts as the Good Shepherd to bring back each little,
lost lamb. As children of God, we are under his watch and
his care. He does not feel as if we are burdens when we
wander, even if we perceive ourselves (or others) that
way. He is led by love in all he does, rejoicing over our
restoration.

May we be filled and led by the same kind of
compassionate care as our wonderful Savior. The Father
doesn't desire for any of his children to be lost, so let's
partner with his purposes and care for the vulnerable
among us who are struggling, disoriented, and wandering.
Instead of reacting to others in judgment, let's let mercy
open our hearts in understanding. What a wonderful world
it would be if we would all follow the example of Christ!

☐ Act of Courage

Choose to help someone today without any ulterior motives.

Surefooted Trust

He is not afraid of bad news;
his heart is firm, trusting in the LORD.

PSALM 112:7 ESV

What would it look like for us to live out this kind of trust? Can you imagine not being afraid of hearing bad news? Though we cannot control what will come with the twists and turns of life, we can be sure the Creator has not changed from yesterday to today. He is the same throughout all the ages, and his powerful mercy is undiminished by time. It is greater than we could ever dream or imagine.

May our hearts be steady and strong, able to calmly face whatever opposes us. May we be generous as our God is generous with us. May our faith be unshaken by even the hardest circumstances. Instead of dreading what is to come, let's raise our expectation to meet the standard of our God's character. He is with us, for us, and ever ready to help us! Why, then, would we be afraid?

 ❏ Act of Courage

Make a list of God's character traits and focus on them every time you are tempted to worry today.

Living Stones

Coming to Him as to a living stone which has been rejected by people, but is choice and precious in the sight of God, you also, as living stones, are being built up as a spiritual house for a holy priesthood, to offer spiritual sacrifices that are acceptable to God through Jesus Christ.

1 PETER 2:4-5 NASB

Jesus Christ is the Living Stone, the one upon whom the church is built. As we come to him as his living stones, we are reflections of his nature because we are in union with him. Let's surrender our lives to his ways, being transformed from the inside out to become more and more like him.

If we walk in the ways of Christ, we are made like him. When his Spirit fills us, we are empowered to face whatever comes. Jesus was rejected, criticized, and crucified, but he never faltered in truth or love. Let's have the courage to follow the example of his love, to stand for justice and mercy, and to go to the places where others refuse to go. Let's refuse to let the opinions of others, known as the fear of man, keep us from living out courageous compassion!

❏ *Act of Courage*

Look to Christ's example for how to live rather than to the expectations of others, even religious people.

Divine Favor

> The king of Egypt liked Joseph and respected him because of the wisdom God gave him. The king made him governor of Egypt and put him in charge of all the people in his palace.
>
> ACTS 7:10 NCV

Though the wisdom of Christ may offend some, it garners respect from others. Think of a time when you saw someone walk in integrity even if it wasn't popular. Did you respect them more for it? A person's character reflects how trustworthy they are. When we walk in the wisdom of God's kingdom, there is an underlying integrity that shines through our lives.

Joseph was faithful with little, and he was faithful with much. He followed through on the ordinary tasks required of him with honor and integrity. This is how he was promoted time and again, not only in his master's house but also by the king of Egypt. Let's not overlook the small and perhaps menial things that are necessary for us to follow through on. If we are faithful with what the Lord gives us, he will give us more.

☐ *Act of Courage*

Don't compare your life with others. Only do what is required of you with honor, follow-through, and an open heart to God's leadership.

Keeping Hope Alive

Quiet your heart in his presence and pray;
keep hope alive as you long for God to come through
for you. And don't think for a moment that the wicked
in their prosperity are better off than you.

PSALM 37:7 TPT

Taking time to quiet our hearts in God's presence
when there is an endless list of things to do can feel
counterintuitive. The truth of the matter, though, is that
when we position our hearts before God and pray, we align
ourselves with his perfect peace. We invite his perspective
to inform our own. Instead of running through our day with
fractured focus, his presence keeps us in the connective
force of his love.

There are times, especially when we are desperate and
waiting, that keeping hope alive feels like a fight against
our own souls. But God will come through. Let's let his
faithfulness inform our expectations instead of letting our
experiences dictate his nature. He is so much better than
we have yet known!

 ☐ *Act of Courage*

*Make pursuing the presence and peace of God your goal
today, all while praying with hope.*

Overcoming Through Christ

Who is he who overcomes the world,
but he who believes that Jesus is the Son of God?

1 JOHN 5:5 NKJV

Every child of God, according to John, overcomes the world through faith. It is faith in Christ that proves to be the magnificent power that triumphs over the world. Let's set our attention on Christ whom Hebrews says is the one who birthed faith within us, and who leads us into faith's perfection (Hebrews 12:2).

Do you long for breakthrough in your life? Set your gaze on Jesus. Persevere in faith, believing he will do that he has said he will do. He will bring light, life, restoration, and redemption. He is capable of much greater things than you could ever ask him. As Ephesians 3:20 says he will outdo even your wildest imagination and unbelievable dreams. Yes, he is that good! In fact, he is even better!

❑ *Act of Courage*

When you are discouraged by the world around you, look to Jesus. He is far better than our weak humanity, and he is close to the brokenhearted.

Forgiven and Restored

"If my people who are called by my name will humble themselves and pray and seek my face and turn from their wicked ways, I will hear from heaven and will forgive their sins and restore their land."

2 CHRONICLES 7:14 NLT

The Lord honors the humble. Jesus offered himself as the example in Matthew 11:29 when he said: "Take my yoke upon you. Let me teach you, because I am humble and gentle at heart, and you will find rest for your souls." Jesus is humble and gentle, and so we should aim to be, as well.

As we humble ourselves before the Lord, we find rest in his forgiveness and restoration. This isn't reserved for some who turn to him, but for all who do! When we open our hearts to the Lord, pray, seek his face, and turn from our self-destructive or self-serving patterns, he not only hears us. He forgives us and restores us! May we have the courage to admit where we are wrong and to change. Let's also be brave enough to offer the same grace to others!

☐ Act of Courage

Admit where you have gotten it wrong,
both to God and to the people in your life.

Set Your Hope

With minds that are alert and fully sober, set your hope on the grace to be brought to you when Jesus Christ is revealed at his coming.

1 PETER 1:13 NIV

As we prepare our minds to be awake to the world around us, we have the opportunity to practice the self-control of the Spirit. It is a fruit of the Spirit for a reason, after all. There is incredible grace in the salvation of Christ which will be revealed as clear as day to the world. Though we are in the interim, waiting on this day, it does not mean God has forgotten.

Let's remember the words of Christ and clothe ourselves in his mercy. Let's let his truth inform our hope. Let's let his example be the only one that matters to us, refusing to compromise our lives with excuses. Verses 15-16 remind us, "just as he who called you is holy, so be holy in all you do; for it is written: 'Be holy, because I am holy.'"

☐ *Act of Courage*

Be intentional with your thoughts today and practice the self-control of the Spirit.

Remember Your Past

Remember that you were a slave in the land of Egypt, and the Lord your God brought you out of there with a strong hand and an outstretched arm. That is why the Lord your God has commanded you to keep the Sabbath day.

DEUTERONOMY 5:15 CSB

Sometimes the courage we need is as accessible as our memory. Think of a time when you were filled with anxiety, only to have it come to rest as everything was resolved. Instead of letting worries about today, tomorrow, or the unknown get the best of you, take a cue from the goodness of God in your experience.

Remember where you came from, what you've survived, and how you've overcome struggles in the past. You may not be able to predict what will happen, but can you trust God will help you and that he's got you? Rest in his peace, and let his presence be what sustains your hope today.

❑ *Act of Courage*

Every time you feel anxiety today, redirect your attention to what is holding you right here and now. Remember God's faithfulness. He will sustain, protect, and help you.

Following in Step

When people's steps follow the LORD,
God is pleased with their ways.
If they stumble, they will not fall,
because the LORD holds their hand.

PSALM 37:23-24 NCV

What does it actually take to follow the Lord? Is it a state of perfection, scholarly knowledge of the Bible, or friendship with God? Moses, Abraham, and David were all known as friends of God. Were they perfect? Far from it! They messed up in various ways and still God called them friends. In their surrender to God, he restored them, time and time again!

Reject the idea that religious perfection is what God is after. It is not. He wants us to know him, to be close to him, and to trust him. He wants to transform our lives with his marvelous mercy as we humble ourselves before him and choose his ways over our own. He is full of loving-kindness, and he does not use our weaknesses against us. Let's follow him and what he requires, humbling ourselves before him and yielding to his Spirit every time we get it wrong.

☐ Act of Courage

Give up trying to appear perfect and simply do your best and love the Lord today.

The Fruit of Perseverance

"The seed in the good soil, these are the ones who have heard the word with a good and virtuous heart, and hold it firmly, and produce fruit with perseverance."

LUKE 8:15 NASB

Endurance is not some extracurricular for faith, but a principle. The fruit of perseverance is life and deliverance. That is what Jesus said in Matthew 24:13, "but the one who endures to the end is the one who will be saved." May we draw courage to keep going, even when the going gets hard.

When we hold firmly to the Word of Christ, letting its power permeate even the deepest parts of our hearts, we are able to endure whatever life throws our way. Perseverance does not mean perfection; we will grow weary. We will need to take time away to rest. Jesus' invitation is an open one for us whenever we need it: "Come to Me, all who are weary and burdened, and I will give you rest" (Matthew 11:28). As we come to him, he refreshes us with the peace of his presence, and we gather the strength we need to persevere.

❏ *Act of Courage*

Before you give up, evaluate whether you just need some time away to rest before continuing.

The Power of Presence

The brothers there, when they heard about us,
came as far as the Forum of Appius and Three Taverns
to meet us. On seeing them, Paul thanked God
and took courage.

ACTS 28:15 ESV

How do you feel after a long-awaited reunion with a good friend? It can be like a shot of dopamine to our systems, bolstering our hope and relieving the energy-sapping, mundane aspects of our lives. Especially in times of great stress, the presence of trusted people can alleviate the weight we carry. Just being near people who love us, know us, and care for us can boost our courage.

Let's be sure we're not prioritizing to-do lists over relationships. Especially for our friends or family members who are struggling, let's take the time to show up in various ways, letting them know we are with them and for them. Let's be purposeful in showing up, knowing it can make a world of difference for their hearts!

☐ Act of Courage

Think of someone you can show up for today.

May

"I have told you this so that you may have peace in me. Here on earth you will have many trials and sorrows. But take heart, because I have overcome the world."

JOHN 16:33 NLT

Helper of the Helpless

LORD, you know the hopes of the helpless.
Surely you will hear their cries and comfort them.

PSALM 10:17 NLT

What person, if they heard the cries of a scared and
hurt child on their own, would not help them? There is
something especially poignant about the helplessness of
children because we know they cannot save themselves,
nor do we expect them to.

At one point did we lose the understanding that, as God's
children, he views us like a loving Father? When we cry out
for help, he rushes in close and comforts us. He soothes us
with his calming presence and offers us the perspective we
need. He knows the hopes of the helpless, and he does not
ignore their cries. He will do for us what we cannot do on our
own, nor does he expect us to! Let's surrender to the peace
of his assistance and lean on him for all we need today.

☐ Act of Courage

Comfort someone who needs help today.

Pray Before Proceeding

"Go, gather together all the Jews who are in Susa, and fast for me. Do not eat or drink for three days, night or day. I and my attendants will fast as you do. When this is done, I will go to the king, even though it is against the law. And if I perish, I perish."

ESTHER 4:15-16 NIV

Esther was in a position to influence the king in an effort to keep the genocide of her people from happening. She did not know how she would be received. She would, after all, be going against his right-hand man, making it his word against her own. Esther needed all the strength she could get, and part of that was a call to some serious prayer.

They fasted and prayed as she prepared to tell the king who she was. When we are overwhelmed by what we know we must do, sometimes the answer is to ask others for prayer support and to take time to prepare our own hearts. Rushing in is usually not necessary. Let's invite others into our process, especially those who may be affected as well. Then, let's proceed when the time comes with courage to face the challenge or difficulty no matter the outcome.

☐ *Act of Courage*

Ask others to pray for you as you prepare to do something that makes you uncomfortable.

Fear of Man

"Don't be afraid of people, who can kill the body but cannot kill the soul. The only one you should fear is the one who can destroy the soul and the body in hell."

MATTHEW 10:28 NCV

How much do we allow the opinions of others to dictate our choices over how we live? We are conditioned to fall in line within the systems of this world, and religious systems are not exempt. Take Jesus' rebuke to the experts of religious law in his own day. These were the powerful and devout of their time. "You make strict rules that are very hard for people to obey, but you yourselves don't even try to follow these rules" (Luke 11:46).

Instead of living under the pressures others put us under, let's live under the liberty Christ has offered us! Galatians 5:1 says, "We have freedom now, because Christ made us free. So, stand strong. Do not change and go back into the slavery of the law." Christ is our Savior and our ultimate leader. Let's follow his liberating mercy and live how he has called us to without fear of what others may think of us!

☐ Act of Courage

Make choices today based on God's leading and your own intuition. Refuse to change based on what others may think of you.

Courageous Contentment

Make sure that your character is free from the love
of money, being content with what you have; for He
Himself has said, "I will never desert you, nor will I ever
abandon you," so that we confidently say, "The LORD is
my helper, I will not be afraid. What will man do to me?"

HEBREWS 13:5-6 NASB

In a world that is constantly trying to get us to buy things
to make us more satisfied, the actual idea of satisfaction is
lost. It is a courageous act to choose contentment! As we
become grateful for what we already have, we are more
able to say no to the things we don't really need. We live in
a very capitalistic society, so it is countercultural to breed
contentment. Let's have the courage to do it, anyway!

It takes intentionality to check in with our own hearts,
minds, and desires. May we not be pulled in directions
without evaluating what is behind it first. May we set up
practices that help us, habits that keep our hearts in check,
and put boundaries around what we mentally ingest.
There is a wonderful kind of peace that is bred in the
contentment of knowing Emmanuel, God with us, is near,
and he will take care of us.

❑ Act of Courage

Don't buy anything unnecessary or unplanned today.

The Way of Jesus

I admit this to you: I worship the God of my ancestors according to the Way, which they call a sect, believing everything that is in accordance with the law and written in the prophets.

ACTS 24:14 CSB

Jesus is the way, the truth, and the life. When we know him, we know the Father. There aren't any hidden paths to get into the kingdom of God. It is through Christ and Christ alone. Let's have the courage to follow his ways, emulate his values, and choose to live out his mercy and kindness to everyone.

The family of God is incredibly inclusive; we don't have to have a certain lifestyle, bank account, or any particular food rules in order to experience his acceptance. Let's be careful not to put extra steps on God's salvation. We are given many choices in the liberty of his love that don't reflect at all on our morality. Let's be people who put first things first, reject the exclusivity of power structures, and worship God in faith and with follow-through.

□ Act of Courage

Put Jesus first, following his example. Let humility be the guard that keeps your heart far from arrogance.

Watch Your Influencers

Follow those who follow wisdom
and stay on the right path.

PROVERBS 2:20 TPT

What we give our attention to, we are filled with. What we are filled with, we become like. Each of us is influenced by others. It's impossible not to be. Do you want to please your parents? Do you want your friends to like your choices? Do you want to be seen as capable, cool, and level-headed? Perhaps none of these things appeal to you. Consider, though, the things that do.

If we want to grow in wisdom, we must listen to those who have wisdom. If we truly want to walk in the light of our Creator and become the best version of who he created us to be, then we will follow through on the wisdom he has set forth. Let's not take for granted where our time and attention go. Is it scrolling through social media? It is in the context of personal relationships that we will truly be seen, grow, and mature. Let's make it a priority to follow those in our own spheres who follow the wisdom of Christ.

☐ *Act of Courage*

Have the courage to proactively use your time!

Perfect Portion

"The LORD is my portion," says my soul,
"therefore I will hope in him."

LAMENTATIONS 3:24 ESV

God is full of generous grace, lavish love, and perfect justice. All he offers comes from the overflow of his very nature. Second Corinthians 9:8 says, "God is able to make all grace abound to you, so that having all sufficiency in all things at all times, you may abound in every good work." He freely offers us all we need through relationship with him.

A scarcity mindset looks at the world as if we are always in the red, and there is not enough to go around. It pushes us to grab hold of the bare minimum and not to let go of it, even for the possibility of better things. This is not the way of God's kingdom, and it doesn't reflect who God is. Let's be brave enough to believe God is as good as he says; he has more than enough grace to offer us for all circumstances, and he wants what is best for us even more than we do!

☐ *Act of Courage*

*Dream bigger today as you take God at his word
and put your hope in him.*

When Heavens Shake

People will be so afraid they will faint, wondering what is happening to the world, because the powers of the heavens will be shaken.

LUKE 21:26 NCV

If we are surprised by the state of the world, we shouldn't be. Jesus, himself, warned that things will get worse, not better, before he returns. Is this a reason to despair? By no means! Does it mean we should abandon hope to see his goodness in the land of the living, as Psalm 27 says? Not at all!

The mercy of God moves in miraculous ways, even in the darkest times. His power is not rendered useless when the world wars against itself. Let's fix our eyes on Jesus, the one who preserves our souls. Let's put our trust in him. Instead of letting evil defeat us, distract us, and lead us to despair, let's defeat evil by doing good (Romans 12:21). Even when people are fainting with fear around us, the firm foundation of our faith remains unshakable!

□ Act of Courage

Continue to do the good you know to do when bad news threatens to overwhelm you. Trust that God is still God!

Wherever You Go

"Have I not commanded you? Be strong and courageous.
Do not be afraid; do not be discouraged, for the LORD
your God will be with you wherever you go."

JOSHUA 1:9 NIV

It is remarkable how many times in the pages of Scripture
God told his people not to fear. We are prone to it! Instead
of trying to run from our fears, let's face them with God
by our side. Courage is having the strength to keep going
even when it feels hard. God did not promise us a mess-
free life, but he certainly did promise to be with us through
it all wherever we go!

Directly before this verse in Joshua, the Lord gave Joshua
some practical advice: "Keep this Book of the Law always
on your lips; meditate on it day and night, so that you may
be careful to do everything written in it." We have even
more than Joshua had then—we have the Holy Spirit within
us to help us. Let's meditate on his Word and cultivate his
presence in our lives.

☐ Act of Courage

*Whatever you are facing today, take the advice of the Lord
and meditate on his Word and trust he is
with you wherever you go!*

No Need to Panic

"Be strong and courageous! Do not be afraid and do not panic before them. For the LORD your God will personally go ahead of you. He will neither fail you nor abandon you."

DEUTERONOMY 31:6 NLT

When God calls you into a situation that makes you feel like you are over your head, don't panic! What he calls you to, he equips you for. He goes before you himself! He will not fail or abandon you. Trust him. Join with the psalmist who said, "I know the Lord is always with me. I will not be shaken, for he is right beside me" (Psalm 16:8).

You will experience the gladness and joy of having God guide you. Your heart will remain at rest in his peace. Take a deep breath, close your eyes, and picture God with you. It is not a fantasy; he is with you! Look to him, reassure your own heart, and walk with him wherever he leads you to go. He is with you through it all, and he will strengthen and uphold you whenever you need him to!

❏ Act of Courage

Take a moment to quiet your mind, take a deep breath and turn your attention to the nearness and greatness of God every time you feel overwhelmed today.

Stay Attentive

Be alert, stand firm in the faith,
be courageous, be strong.

1 CORINTHIANS 16:13 CSB

It is an important thing to pay attention not only to our own lives and feelings, to those of the people around us, and also to what is happening in the world around us. As we remain observant, let us also keep in mind the greatness and power of God. He has not changed, and he never will. His resurrection power is as potent today as it was when Christ rose from the grave. As we consider him, he infuses his strength within us.

Even as we build a habit of watchfulness, let's not neglect what Paul said next in his letter to the Corinthians. He said love and kindness should be the motivation behind all we do. Even as we are paying attention, we should lead with love. We can recognize the signs of the times and the harsh realities around us but still hold on to loyal love without letting go. So, stay attentive, but stay attentive with love as your motivation.

☐ *Act of Courage*

Be intentional about reading from different news sources, talking to different people, and broadening your perspective today.

One Prevailing Thing

I ask only one thing from the LORD.
This is what I want:
Let me live in the LORD's house all my life.
Let me see the LORD's beauty and look with my own
eyes at his Temple.

PSALM 27:4 NCV

We can look with courage beyond the pull of passing desires and into the face of the one who knows us best. When we get a taste of his marvelous love, it becomes less of a courageous choice and more of a burning passion. Psalm 34:8 says we should taste and see that the Lord is good. "Happy is the person who trusts him."

What would it look like for you to turn your attention to him today? What would you need to sacrifice? What would you need to adjust? Just one glimpse is all it takes to transform our hearts and expand our understanding. One glimpse of God's glory, and we will know we were created for so much more than we have settled for. Let's readjust our vision as we look to him today!

☐ *Act of Courage*

Look to the Lord as often as it comes to mind today.
Ask him to reveal his glory to you in new ways!

Way of Escape

No temptation has overtaken you except something common to mankind; and God is faithful, so He will not allow you to be tempted beyond what you are able, but with the temptation will provide the way of escape also, so that you will be able to endure it.

1 CORINTHIANS 10:13 NASB

The Lord provides us with grace and strength when we need it. In the face of temptation there is always a way of escape. Do we trust the Lord to help us? Do we look for the ways he offers us to grow in endurance? His mercy is ever so near, and he does not ignore us when we cry out to him for help.

It takes courage to resist temptation. With integrity and the empowering grace of God, we can exercise the fruit of self-control. Let's strengthen our souls as we can, not letting little compromises weaken our resolve. There is a wealth of wisdom in following the Lord and his ways. Let's not forget that!

☐ Act of Courage

Ask the Lord for help and for an alternative way when you face a temptation today.

Precious Confidence

Guilty criminals experience paranoia even though no one threatens them. But the innocent lovers of God, because of righteousness, will have the boldness of a young, ferocious lion!

PROVERBS 28:1 TPT

When we walk in the light as God is in the light, we have nothing to hide. In other words, when we live with honesty, mercy, and intentionality, we can confidently continue without fear of being found out. Even if others throw accusations our way, if they are unfounded, justice will be on our side.

The guilty are paranoid even when no threat is present. Be cautious therefore, of those who seem to always have a defensive tone. When we walk in the love of God, mercy covers our steps. There is no need to ridicule, blame, or shame others. Let's rise up in the confidence of our position in Christ. He has purified us from all unrighteousness and made us clean in his sight! Let's live, therefore, with the integrity of his values on display in our lives.

☐ Act of Courage

Don't let fear cause you to lash out at others; rather, ask God for his perspective over the things that cause you worry.

Authentic Living

Only let your manner of life be worthy of the gospel of Christ, so that whether I come and see you or am absent, I may hear of you that you are standing firm in one spirit, with one mind striving side by side for the faith of the gospel, and not frightened in anything by your opponents.

PHILIPPIANS 1:27-28 ESV

When we live with the reality of the gospel of Christ as our guide, it shines through our actions. Let's clothe ourselves in the love of Jesus, which is more wonderful than the allowances of human affection. It is powerful, full of justice, and transforms us from the inside out.

How important is authenticity to you? Have you learned to be yourself around all kinds of people? Though we may show slightly different sides to some, who we are at our core does not change. May we have the courage to show up as ourselves, all while allowing the transformative grace of God to continue to lead us into growth.

 ☐ *Act of Courage*

Choose the way of Christ over your own preferences when confronted with the opportunity. For example, extend grace rather than lashing out in anger.

Successful Partnership

> Then you will succeed if you carefully follow the statutes and ordinances the LORD commanded Moses for Israel. Be strong and courageous. Don't be afraid or discouraged.
>
> 1 CHRONICLES 22:13 CSB

A couple of verses before David made this statement to his son, Solomon, he said, "My son, the Lord be with you, so that you may succeed in building the house of the Lord your God." Success is more than achievement. It is partnership with God. It is through God's help we are able to do what he has called us to do. This remains as true today as it did then.

Following the Lord is much more than abiding by rules and regulations. It is knowing him, befriending him, and reflecting him. Nothing is impossible with God. No matter what we are called to, we are able to do it with the help of God as our partner! Let's be sure to make our relationship with him a priority. We know what to do when we listen to the one who walks with us!

❏ Act of Courage

Ask the Lord to lead you in your decisions today, and partner with his character, even if you struggle to hear his voice.

Daily Reminders

I have set the Lord always before me;
Because He is at my right hand I shall not be moved.

PSALM 16:8 NKJV

Are you a visual person? Perhaps you like to write lists in which you can check off the tasks as they are accomplished. Maybe you like to have pictures of your loved ones around. How could it help you if you were to put reminders of the Lord and his character in places that are easy to spot?

Choose a verse, a word, an attribute, or a picture that encapsulates something about the Lord that is meaningful to you. Put it in a place where you will see it often, and every time you notice it take a moment to pray. It doesn't have to be a long prayer. Just turn your attention to God, thanking him for being by your side. What courage will grow within you as you do!

□ *Act of Courage*

Share what reminder you have chosen with a friend and tell them what you are doing.

Discerning and Innocent

"Look, I am sending you out as sheep among wolves. So be as shrewd as snakes and harmless as doves. But beware! For you will be handed over to the courts and will be flogged with whips in the synagogues. You will stand trial before governors and kings because you are my followers. But this will be your opportunity to tell the rulers and other unbelievers about me."

MATTHEW 10:16-18 NLT

Jesus did not call us to be gullible, but he also didn't call us to stand in judgment against others. Let's couple wisdom with innocence, being sure to use discernment, for it will save us from many disappointments.

Even as we grow in discernment, let's be sure to not cause harm to others. Many use the discernment they gain to build walls around themselves. But Jesus did not call us to build barriers where he broke them down. Sometimes the very thing he calls us into is the troubles of this world. May we remain steadfast, following his example. He did not promise us lives of ease, but he did promise us the peace of his presence that goes with us!

☐ Act of Courage

Don't turn a blind eye to the harsh realities in the world. Let them challenge you, but don't give in to despair.

Purposeful Peace

"Peace I leave with you; my peace I give you. I do not give to you as the world gives. Do not let your hearts be troubled and do not be afraid."

JOHN 14:27 NIV

Peace brokered by powers in the world is not lasting; it is fragile. It is subject to the whims of nations, the greed of power-hungry leaders, and economic trade-offs. This is not cynical. It is true! Jesus said he does not give peace the way the world does. This is incredibly good news. His peace is lasting, and it is not dependent on the circumstances surrounding us.

The Holy Spirit has been given to us, he sets us free, and he permeates us with the peace of Christ. What Jesus offered, he also offers. What the Father is full of, the Spirit gives us. There is no better relief than the peace of Christ which dwells within us. Let's not take this for granted, for it is an abundantly generous gift!

□ Act of Courage

Ask the Holy Spirit to fill you with the peace of Christ that passes understanding today.

Joyful Trust

I pray that the God who gives hope will fill you with much joy and peace while you trust in him. Then your hope will overflow by the power of the Holy Spirit.

ROMANS 15:13 NCV

God is a fountain of hope and overflowing inspiration. Whatever you long for is found completely in him. Whatever you need, he has in abundance! May you stand under the waterfall of his grace today, soaking in the pleasure of his presence and the life-giving power of his love. It is much easier to trust someone you know well, so don't neglect the importance of spending time getting to know him more. He is not stingy with his wisdom, nor is he too busy to meet you every moment you turn to him.

Joyful trust is a result of experiencing his faithfulness in our lives. Our hope overflows as we witness his marvelous mercy moving in our lives and on our behalf. He is so much better than we could ever give him credit for, so let's lean into his luxurious love today!

☐ Act of Courage

Ask the Holy Spirit to fill your awareness with the tangible love of his presence.

Lay Them Down

In the day that I'm afraid, I lay all my fears before you and trust in you with all my heart. What harm could a man bring to me? With God on my side I will not be afraid of what comes. The roaring praises of God fill my heart, and I will always triumph as I trust his promises.

PSALM 56:3-4 TPT

I love this psalm. David is honest about his fear. He doesn't deny that he grapples with it, nor does he ignore that he will experience it in the future. No, he says, "But in the day that I'm afraid, I lay all my fears before you." This is a powerful act! In his helplessness, he gives all that he cannot control to God. He lays them out before him.

Sometimes, we need to remind ourselves who God is. When we compare his greatness with the objects of our fear, he wins out every time! With God on our side, we do not need to fear what comes. Let's use even our fears to fuel our worship. That's what David did; when his fear got loud, his praise got louder. Let's try it for ourselves and see what happens!

❏ Act of Courage

Lay your fears before God as you experience them. When you feel helpless, give the reins to the Lord and trust him.

Walking on Water

He said, "Come!" And Peter got out of the boat and walked on the water, and came toward Jesus.

MATTHEW 14:29 NASB

If you saw one of your close friends doing something that seemed impossible and they invited you to join them, would you? Jesus was the Son of God, and we know this. Yet to Peter, he was a teacher, friend, and companion. It took courage for Peter to step out of the boat onto the water where Jesus was walking. Notice that no one else got out of the boat!

Will we have the courage to step out into situations that seem dangerous when Jesus calls us to come join him? We know the rest of the story. Peter got overwhelmed by the water around him, became frightened, began to sink, and cried out for help. Even in his doubt, Jesus was there to help him, even if he did call him out on it. Let's have the courage to step out in faith and trust God to sustain us there!

☐ Act of Courage

When you feel God's invitation to something new and scary, take a step of faith and join him.

Our Confidence

What, then, are we to say about these things? If God is
for us, who is against us? He did not even spare his own
Son but gave him up for us all. How will he not also with
him grant us everything?

ROMANS 8:31-32 CSB

No matter what life throws our way, God promises that
nothing can ever separate us from his great love. Not
hardship or storm. Not war or famine. The God who
created the universe with his words, speaks life to us right
where we are at.

May we find our great confidence, not in our comfort or
the peace of this world, but in Christ himself. May we look
to him no matter what is happening around us. There is
perfect peace in his presence. There is abundant affection
in his heart. There is jubilant joy in his victory. There is
more than enough to sustain us and revive us in hope in his
generous grace and mercy!

☐ *Act of Courage*

*Memorize this verse and recite it whenever
you need a boost of courage today!*

Continuous Access

Seek the Lord and his strength;
seek his presence continually!

1 CHRONICLES 16:11 ESV

This stanza is from a song of thanksgiving which David offered the worshipers, the Levites, who presided over the Ark of the Lord. As we worship the Lord, we are to search for him. He is easily found! He has given us open access through his Spirit. We don't have to go to a specified place or relic in order to worship the King of kings. This is incredibly liberating and humbling news.

Wherever you are today, take time to worship the Lord. Whether it is through meditation, singing, walking in nature, or dancing before him; whatever form your worship takes, make it an offering that flows from your heart to his. The Lord says in Jeremiah 29:13, "You will seek me and find me, when you seek me with all your heart." Look for him, and you will find him.

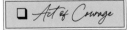
☐ Act of Courage

Spend time today in dedicated worship to the Lord. Offer him your heart, no matter what your worship looks like.

Call to Action

"Get up, for it is your duty to tell us how to proceed in setting things straight. We are behind you, so be strong and take action."

Ezra 10:4 NLT

When we are discouraged, we can easily forget the roles we fill, whether they are those of friend, worker, daughter, or son, and their importance. It takes courage to recognize and rise up in our specific roles when we are burned out. There is a time for rest, and there is a time for action, sometimes cycling through both in the same day.

Let's have the boldness to build rhythms of both rest and action into our lives. Let's not neglect the space we need to refresh, but let's also not forsake the responsibilities that are ours to fulfill. It takes discernment, endurance, and outside perspective to propel us sometimes. May we listen to those who are behind us, cheering us on toward growth and joining with us in the pursuit of greater liberation in Christ's love.

☐ Act of Courage

Whenever you feel stuck today, ask for perspective from others around you and ask for the Lord to give you the grace to empower you.

Eternal Pleasures

We are confident, yes, well pleased rather to be absent
from the body and to be present with the Lord.

2 CORINTHIANS 5:8 NKJV

This one, short life we live in the flesh is not the end. For
believers in Christ, we look forward to an eternity spent in
the beauty of his forever kingdom. The one who is outside
of time is the one we will join when we leave our failing
frames and receive our eternal bodies.

May we have the courage to live with confidence founded
in faith and may our ultimate hope swell within us as we
focus on the beauty that awaits us in the fullness of God's
kingdom. Whether we live or die, as Paul went on to say
in this chapter, may we make it our life's passion to live to
please God. Nothing we do in this life is overlooked. Every
subtle surrender and motivation is accounted for. Let's live
under and for his mercy, justice, and peace!

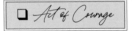
❏ Act of Courage

When you are discouraged by the state of affairs around
you, think about the wonderful glory that lies ahead where
there will be no more sorrow, separation, or pain.

Trust God

> Then Joshua said to them, "Do not be afraid, nor be dismayed; be strong and of good courage, for thus the LORD will do to all your enemies against whom you fight."

JOSHUA 10:25 NCV

Every oath, promise, and vow that the Lord makes, he follows through on. There is so much mystery in his ways; who can truly understand him? But his character never changes through it all. Do we trust him to accompany us as he calls us? Do we trust that he will truly never leave or abandon us?

There is no better way to build our trust with God than to get to know what he is like. We have his character, the recorded miracles of Jesus, and the Holy Spirit to teach us. Let's look to the Lord when we are confused. Let's trust his faithful nature rooted in loving-kindness and true justice and stand upon the foundation of his presence. Let's be strong and of good courage, taking the Lord at his reliable word!

☐ Act of Courage

Write down the character traits of God which cause your heart to hope, your faith to grow, and your peace to expand.

Perfect Love's Force

There is no fear in love. But perfect love drives out fear,
because fear has to do with punishment. The one who
fears is not made perfect in love.

1 JOHN 4:18 NIV

God is a good Father. He does not barter in fear or control
us with manipulation. He does not punish us for our
humanity. He loves us to life, even when pointing out our
flaws. He is infinitely kind, patient, and wonderful. His truth-
telling is not flattery. He is able to correct us in kindness,
revealing a higher perspective and calling us to rise up to it.

Have you ever felt bolstered by another's love for you?
Do you know the security of love that allows for differing
opinions without them being threats to your connection
with others? Perfect love drives out fear. Perfect love
does not ignore the needs of others; it looks for ways to
meet them. When we truly grasp the love God has given
us through Christ, loving others becomes our grateful
response!

☐ Act of Courage

*When you are tempted to shut down from someone close
to you today, choose to extend love and curiosity instead.*

United in Purpose

Whatever happens, keep living your lives based on the reality of the gospel of Christ, which reveals him to others. Then when I come to see you, or hear good reports of you, I'll know that you stand united in one Spirit and one passion—celebrating together as conquerors in the faith of the gospel.

PHILIPPIANS 1:27 TPT

No matter what happens, no matter where you live, what community you are a part of, or what church you do or do not attend, the reality of the gospel of Christ does not change. Make that your focus—the gospel of Christ—and you have a firm foundation beneath your feet.

The uniting passion of believers should, in fact, be Jesus Christ. If it is not, then we have lost our focus of what Jesus came to reveal about God, what he desires for us, and the expansive love of his heart and kingdom. May we keep our eyes on Jesus, follow his example, and choose the often harder and smaller path of life that opts for mercy over revenge, sacrifice over self-promotion, and integrity over success.

❏ Act of Courage

Simplify your faith by looking to the life, ministry, teaching, and presence of Jesus as your guide, rather than all the extra things so often put upon it.

Truth Tellers

"He has only human strength, but we have the LORD our God to help us and to fight our battles." So the people relied on the words of King Hezekiah of Judah.

2 CHRONICLES 32:8 CSB

We need encouragement to bolster our courage and to refine our vision. We need people who are willing to tell the truth even when it is inconvenient. We need people of wisdom who know the heart of the Lord to remind us of his faithfulness. On good days, we may be more apt to lean into the goodness of God. In seasons of suffering, we may require frequent input and encouragement.

True encouragement is based in truth, not in flattery. It touches the depths of our hearts, going beyond the surface of our egos. May we be people who know and walk with the Lord so closely that we are able to remind others of his strength and faithfulness when they forget. May we benefit from the perceptive wisdom of those around us who have received the revelation of the strength and goodness of God.

❏ *Act of Courage*

Share what God has encouraged your own heart in with someone today.

Life Lessons

Here's what I've learned through it all:
Don't give up; don't be impatient;
be entwined as one with the Lord. Be brave and
courageous, and never lose hope.
Yes, keep on waiting—for he will never disappoint you!

PSALM 27:14 TPT

What is this "all" David alludes to in this verse? Psalm 27 is a poem of praise to God before David was anointed king. Even in hardship while others were seeking to harm him, David garnered his courage from God. He trusted God to guard him, to keep him, and to lead him into his triumph. He gave himself to learning from God how to live and to walk in wisdom and courage.

What would it look like for us to become entwined with the Lord as David suggested? When we wait upon him, trusting him to come through for us, and resting in his presence, that is where we become brave and courageous, holding on to hope. The God who did not disappoint David even in troubles of his own making, and God will not disappoint us as we lean on him for all we need.

❏ Act of Courage

Take time in prayer, even in silence, opening your heart before the Lord and asking the Holy Spirit to move in you, increasing your peace, and meeting all the needs you have.

June

Be strong, and let your heart take courage, all you who wait for the Lord!

Psalm 31:24 ESV

Wonderful Promise

The Spirit of the LORD will rest on Him, The spirit of wisdom and understanding, The spirit of counsel and strength, The spirit of knowledge and the fear of the LORD.

ISAIAH 11:2 NASB

There is so much goodness in the grace of God's Spirit with us. Isaiah prophesied about the Messiah long before Jesus was born, lived, died, and was resurrected from the grave to ascend to the right hand of his Father in heaven. He spoke of the Spirit of the Lord resting upon him, empowering him in all sorts of ways. This Spirit, we know, was the same Holy Spirit whom Jesus promised would come upon his people after he returned to his throne.

In John 14:16-17, Jesus said, "I will ask the Father, and He will give you another Helper, so that He may be with you forever; the Helper is the Spirit of truth." The Spirit of wisdom and understanding, of counsel and strength, of knowledge and the fear of the Lord, is the Spirit who rests upon *us* today. What a beautiful gift!

☐ *Act of Courage*

Ask the Holy Spirit to teach you from the wealth of God's wisdom today, and every time it comes to mind, ask again!

Sit at Wisdom's Feet

I have counsel and sound wisdom;
I have insight; I have strength.

PROVERBS 8:14 ESV

Are you looking for insight? The Spirit of Wisdom has discernment into wise plans which are specifically designed for you! Your Creator did not simply form you and then leave you. You have an open invitation into his presence through his Spirit whom he offers to you through Christ! He has solutions for the problems that exasperate you. He will guide you as you look to him, even when you cannot see what is two steps ahead.

The book of Proverbs is full of invitations to follow Wisdom and her ways. She will not steer you wrong, nor will she trick you. She has good counsel and sound wisdom, insight, and strength. With her is true success. Trust the wisdom of God. Follow through and you will find that even when you could not understand why, there was purpose in her directives.

☐ Act of Courage

*Before you jump into any decision today,
either big or small, ask the Holy Spirit to direct you
in the ways that are best for you.*

Just One Touch

Then the one who looked like a man touched me again, and I felt my strength returning. "Don't be afraid," he said, "for you are very precious to God. Peace! Be encouraged! Be strong!" As he spoke these words to me, I suddenly felt stronger and said to him, "Please speak to me, my lord, for you have strengthened me."

DANIEL 10:18-19 NLT

One touch is all it takes for our strength to return. One touch of God's presence, and we are revived. There is no situation where we are without his Spirit, so let's remember to call on him and turn our attention to him throughout our day.

However weak you feel today, the Spirit of God is near. Ask for the power of his presence to touch your body, mind, heart, and spirit now. Hear him as he says, "Don't be afraid, for you are very precious to God." Be encouraged by his love for you!

☐  Act of Courage

Ask God to touch any part of your life that feels weak.
Ask him to speak directly to your heart today
and take time to listen for his voice.

Reach Out

> Just then a woman who had been subject to bleeding for twelve years came up behind him and touched the edge of his cloak. She said to herself, "If I only touch his cloak, I will be healed."
>
> MATTHEW 9:20-21 NIV

Jesus credited this brave woman for her faith. He literally felt power seep from his person when she simply touched the edge of his robe; can you imagine? She didn't even touch his body! Yet it was this simple, humble, and incredibly bold act that led to her healing. When Jesus turned around, he told the woman, "Take heart, daughter, your faith has healed you" (verse 22).

Have you been tormented by something for longer than you ever imagined you would be? Reach out in faith to your Savior today. Touch the hem of his garment with the movement of your heart. He is more than able to meet you, heal you, restore you, and encourage you in hope. May he flood you with the incredible peace of his presence!

☐ *Act of Courage*

Take a step of bold faith today.

Always and Forever

God is our protection and our strength.
He always helps in times of trouble.

PSALM 46:1 NCV

Whenever we need help, God is there. He is reliable in love, and he is persistent in grace. We are never without him! Why would we look to find refuge anywhere else when the Rock of Ages is our proven protection and strength? May we turn to him with all of our needs, asking for his help and giving him our devotion.

Even if the world around us crumbles, God remains the same Mighty God who moves mountains and preserves the innocent. Let's not give up hope when life gets hard. Let's press into the presence of God, looking to him more than ever. How well do we know him? How much trust do we put in his unfailing nature? Let's meditate on his goodness even when we struggle to see it in our present reality. He is ever so near, and his mercies are still new every morning.

*Turn to God with every need you have today,
even the littlest ones!*

Sure-Footed

The LORD my Lord is my strength;
he makes my feet like those of a deer
and enables me to walk on mountain heights!

HABAKKUK 3:19 CSB

Mountaintops are really romantic to think about, but they
are also quite dangerous. It is a long, arduous journey
to climb a mountain. Especially near the top it can be
rocky and difficult to stay on your feet. The air is thinner,
the climate is cooler, and the terrain is more difficult to
traverse. But God, the Lord, is our strength. He makes our
feet able to tread upon the heights as we trust in the God
of our salvation.

Perhaps this reminder that God readies our feet even as we
wait on him is what we need to get through the challenges
that face us today. Let's turn our attention to God, our
Savior, and trust he is moving even when we cannot sense
him. He steadies us as we follow him. He is right beside us!

*When you feel as if you are sliding and slipping,
ask the Lord to hold you up! Ask for his perspective of
the circumstances you find yourself in.*

Prosperous Fruit

Beloved ones, stand firm and secure. Live your lives with an unshakable confidence. We know that we prosper and excel in every season by serving the Lord, because we are assured that our union with the Lord makes our labor productive with fruit that endures.

1 Corinthians 15:58 tpt

All we do has an effect. Our choices build us in a direction. Are we aware of that? Do we have intentionality about what we do with our time, resources, and relationships? Or are we coasting in the mundane of the day-to-day? Life has all sorts of ebbs and flows, so we cannot expect to always be propelling forward. Some days look more like maintenance, and that's okay.

As we grow closer to the Lord through fellowship with his Spirit, we get to partner with his purposes. Let's focus on building that relationship, following his leadership in our lives, and aligning with his kingdom values as we live. We will bear beautiful fruit as we abide in the vine of his love!

☐ Act of Courage

Write down what values of Christ's kingdom you want your choices to reflect and use it as a guide for your decision-making.

Sacred Imagination

The steadfast of mind You will keep in perfect peace,
Because he trusts in You.

ISAIAH 26:3 NASB

Our imaginations are a gift from God. Christ sanctifies our thoughts as well as our imaginations, and we can partner with his purposes even in in the landscape of our minds! Have you ever considered that you could use your imagination to increase your faith, to meet the Lord, or to dream with God?

There is a deep well of peace in the presence of God, and it dwells with those who have yielded to his leadership. Our mindsets frame our reality. May we submit our thoughts to Christ and allow the Spirit to teach us, enlarge our understanding, and transform our expectations. As we dream with the Lord and are grounded in his truth, our hearts grow strong roots of trust. May we not neglect the beauty and wonder of our sacred imaginations!

❏ Act of Courage

Close your eyes, ask the Lord to sanctify your mind, and allow your imagination to lead you into deeper fellowship with him.

Peaceful Fruit of Integrity

When a man's ways please the LORD,
He makes even his enemies to be at peace with him.

PROVERBS 16:7 NKJV

The grace of God is ready to empower you to turn enemies into friends. How is this possible? When you walk in the light of God's love, choosing integrity, mercy, kindness, and justice in your decisions and interactions, even those who do not agree with you will have nothing they can truly fault you for. Don't get caught up in people pleasing, but set your heart on what honors God, and do those things.

Instead of seeking to appease others, focus on pleasing God. Get to know him more, reading his Word and fellowshipping with his Spirit. Spend time in his presence, consider his nature, and align your heart with his values. Allow his wisdom to guide you, even when it feels as if it goes against your logic. His understanding is faultless, and he will not lead you astray.

☐ *Act of Courage*

*Be true to who God has called you to be,
and be kind to others even when they are
unkind toward you.*

Completely Covered

It was faith that immersed you into Jesus,
the Anointed One, and now you are
covered and clothed with his anointing.

GALATIANS 3:27 TPT

As true children of God, which is anyone who believes in Jesus as the Anointed One, we can confidently come to the throne of our Father without shame or hesitation. The anointing of Christ covers us completely. It is through Christ, and Christ alone, that we enter into the courts of our God as pure and blameless children of the Most High.

That same faith that immersed us into his kingdom is the faith that propels us in perseverance to continue to choose the ways of Christ as we live. What God has forgiven us for and released us from, may we not take up again. What he has freed others from, may we not hold against them. Let's walk in the strength-giving grace of God which allows for new starts, patient endurance, and follow-through. We are completely covered, no matter what we need!

If there is something holding you back in fear, shame, or uncertainty, bring it to Jesus today. Lay it out before him and allow him to clothe you with his mercy.

Power to Continue

> When they had prayed, the place in which they were gathered together was shaken, and they were all filled with the Holy Spirit and continued to speak the word of God with boldness.

ACTS 4:31 ESV

Before Jesus ascended to heaven leaving his followers to continue his ministry, he said to them: "Behold, I am sending the promise of my Father upon you. But stay in the city until you are clothed with power from on high" (Luke 24:49). The first chapter of Acts expands on this even more, recounting Jesus' words when he said, "for John baptized with water, but you will be baptized with the Holy Spirit not many days from now" (Acts 1:5).

Have you ever experienced the power of the Holy Spirit in your own being? Jesus promised the Holy Spirit would come upon his people, filling them with the power of God. If you haven't known this to be true for you, ask him to do it! Then wait upon him. The Spirit of God is not fickle and does not need perfect conditions. He is with you. Ask him to open your eyes, ears, and heart to him!

☐ Act of Courage

Ask the Lord to fill you with a fresh encounter of his power through his Holy Spirit!

Sharing in Victory

Thank God! He gives us victory over sin and death through our Lord Jesus Christ.

1 CORINTHIANS 15:57 NLT

"Death is swallowed up in victory." This Scripture is what Paul recalled before going on to say that Christ has given us victory over sin and death! The sting of death has been dulled by the triumph of our Savior. He fulfilled the Law and was the pure, spotless Lamb of God, offered for the sins of the whole world. Through him, we have full forgiveness!

Thank God for his power to save. What a wonder that he gave his own Son to set us free from the curse of sin and death. What courage we can take in this—what hope! There is nothing we have done or could ever do that would nullify Christ's victory. His mercy is strong enough to cover every sin. Let's share the good news of his marvelous grace with those in our lives, and let's encourage them to look for the power of God's mercy toward them!

☐ *Act of Courage*

Thank the Lord for specific things from which he has forgiven and freed you.

Liberty of Belonging

The Spirit you received does not make you slaves, so that you live in fear again; rather, the Spirit you received brought about your adoption to sonship. And by him we cry, "Abba, Father."

ROMANS 8:15 NIV

Have you ever been a part of a group whose members made you feel like an outsider? Perhaps when you started a new school, joined a new club, or moved to a new place, you felt the vulnerability of not being seen, known, or accepted. Is this how you feel with God, or do you know him as your tender and caring Father? Do you know how precious you are to him? Do you know the beat of his heart and trust the wisdom of his correction?

In the kingdom of God, we are family, not outsiders. Not one of us is an outcast in his eyes. He draws in the lonely, and he covers them with the life-giving love of his heart. He is not far-off. He is close, attentive, and incredibly patient. He understands us more fully than we could imagine. Let's lean into his presence and leave behind the fear of being rejected.

☐ Act of Courage

Choose to push past the fear of doing something with people who don't know you well, and know that God, who knows you best, is with you wherever you go!

Sweet Surrender

A man's steps are ordained by the LORD;
How then can a person understand his way?

PROVERBS 20:24 NASB

So much of our lives remain a mystery to us. Our futures unfold as we take each step. We may know the direction we are heading, but we don't know the twists and turns that will occur along the way. We cannot foresee every challenge that will meet us nor the unexpected joys we will experience.

With that in mind, it is a comfort to know the Lord sees the end from the beginning and every space in-between. He already knows what lies ahead of us, and we can trust him to guide us along every hill and through every valley. The God who knows how many hairs are on each of our heads will not forget about us. May we humble ourselves in sweet surrender, trusting that the Lord who created us will lead us with love!

☐ *Act of Courage*

Surrender your worries about the future to the Lord and ask him for vision and help for today.

Eyes of Faith

> Say to people who are frightened, "Be strong. Don't be afraid. Look, your God will come, and he will punish your enemies. He will make them pay for the wrongs they did, but he will save you."
>
> ISAIAH 35:4 NCV

God is a God of justice. We may wait for him to move, but he will do it. He will make all wrong things right and bring restoration to his people, as well as to the earth. When we are discouraged by the chaos of the world, let us look to him – the one who is full of glory, grace, and mercy. He draws us in with loving-kindness, and he sustains our hope with his incomparable love.

Sometimes, we need the reminder that God isn't finished yet. He has not forgotten his promises, nor has he given up on us. Let's rejoice in his love that is available, right here and right now. Let's breathe in the peace of his presence, turning our minds and our hearts to him like sunflowers tilt toward the sun to soak up its life-giving energy. Let us look with eyes of faith, knowing Christ has already conquered the grave, and he will come again to restore the earth and everything in it.

Read through the promises of God and let your heart take courage in faith.

Answers of Strength

On the day I called, you answered me;
you increased strength within me.

PSALM 138:3 CSB

A swift answer can bring both relief and strength as David described in this psalm. Have you ever prayed for an answer, a need, or an insight and received what you asked for within the same day? Though this is not always how God works; he does not delay without reason. When we receive his help in tangible ways it is a great boost to our courage!

When God comes through for us, let's share that goodness with others! Let's not hold back from sharing our own relief with others for our shared encouragement. Let's be sure to offer help too when we are able. Our own offerings can be the very answer to others' prayers! Let us consider, then, how we might share our joys with others in a variety of ways.

☐ *Act of Courage*

*Help someone who reaches out to you today if
you are able, even if it is a small act!*

Eyes to See

Immediately Jesus spoke to them, saying,
"Take heart; it is I. Do not be afraid."

MATTHEW 14:27 ESV

Often when we read the story of Jesus walking on the water, we think of Peter and his experience as he joined Jesus there. What of the other disciples? When they all first spotted Jesus walking on top of the water, it did not make sense to them; they thought he was a ghost! They were overcome with terror as many of us would be in their same position. However, Jesus encouraged them to be brave and to not be afraid, assuring them that it was him that was walking toward them.

Fear can do strange things to our minds. It can shift our expectations, mess with our perceptions, and cause our nervous systems to heighten. The disciples were already afraid because of the storm that had overcome their boat. Seeing the figure of a man walking on the water just took it over the top. Jesus walks through the middle of our own storms to meet us. Let's take hope in his presence, and let's accept the peace he offers as he says, "Take heart; it is I."

❑ Act of Courage

Ask Jesus to break through your fear with his presence!

Lush Pastures

Ask the LORD for rain in the spring, for he makes the storm clouds. And he will send showers of rain so every field becomes a lush pasture.

ZECHARIAH 10:1 NLT

Though the seasons come and go without our prodding—indeed, even sometimes without our notice—there is an invitation written within the rhythms of the seasons to welcome God into our experiences. Ask the Lord for rain in the spring so every field bears the abundant harvest of a lush year. Rain brings relief in times of drought. It brings life and nourishment to the dry land.

Are there any dry areas in your own life? Ask the Lord to send the rain of his Spirit over you. He who makes the storm clouds also makes the air you breathe. He washes over you with the relentlessly refreshing waves of his presence. Your life will become a lush pasture of his mercy as you drink in the nourishment of his peace.

☐ *Act of Courage*

Ask the Lord for what you need from him.
Nothing is too insignificant, and nothing is too great.
Ask it all!

He Is the One

"The LORD, He is the One who goes before you. He will be with you, He will not leave you nor forsake you; do not fear nor be dismayed."

DEUTERONOMY 31:8 NKJV

Have you ever been overwhelmed by a seemingly impossible task that lies ahead of you? Perhaps it looks like a transition into new responsibilities you aren't sure you're equipped for. Maybe it is a prodigious circumstance you cannot avoid or escape. Instead of getting caught up in the unknowns you cannot control, lean into this moment and into who God has been, who he is, and who he will continue to be.

The Lord is already ahead of you preparing the way. He is also with you, transcending time and space to inhabit every moment. You are his child, and he will not abandon you. Don't give into the fear that he will leave you, for he promises he never will! By his Spirit, he is with you at all times. You are never without him!

☐ *Act of Courage*

When you feel your mind getting ahead of yourself, ask God to reveal his presence to you.

Anchor of Hope

You will be secure, because there is hope;
you will look about you and take your rest in safety.

JOB 11:18 NIV

Having hope gives us courage. We are able to rest in the peace of God's presence knowing he will not leave us. Hebrews 6:19 says, "We have this hope as an anchor for the soul, firm and secure." This strong, unbreakable hope is fastened to Jesus Christ. We throw our anchor into the ocean of his vast love.

Do you know the security of this hope? Do you know your prayers keep you connected to the heart of your father like a rope holds an anchor? Don't dismay when you experience pain. Know that it is temporary as are all things in this fleeting life. Put all your expectations on God like you're placing a sure bet. He will not let you down, and he will not leave you alone!

❑ *Act of Courage*

Connect to the hope of your soul through an open line of prayer throughout your day, like an ongoing conversation you keep coming back to.

Prepared to Fight

David said to Saul, "Don't let anyone be discouraged.
I, your servant, will go and fight this Philistine!"

1 Samuel 17:32 NCV

David already had faith that God could and would defeat
the Philistines before he stood before Saul. The Israeli army
was not so confident; they were afraid of the giant, Goliath.
David was just a shepherd boy at this point, and that's
all the experience he had. But he had seen God deliver
him from being killed by a lion and a bear. In fact, he had
overtaken and killed both. With that experience under his
belt! He was sure God would do the same with the giant!

How many of us despise the seasons when we are alone
and seemingly insignificant? The truth is, without learning
to know God in the pastures while tending and caring
for his father's sheep, David may not have had the same
confidence. God uses our training seasons to propel us into
where he has called us. With faith in God and experience
facing the challenges of our lives under our belt, we will be
able to face greater obstacles with unabashed boldness.

☐ *Act of Courage*

*When you see someone else in need of help
and you have the faith to step in, do it!*

Constant Watch

"Keep a constant watch over your soul, and pray for the courage and grace to prevail over these things that are destined to occur and that you will stand before the presence of the Son of Man with a clear conscience."

LUKE 21:36 TPT

Life is unpredictable. We do not know when we will draw our last breath or when our hearts will stop beating. We should live then, like this is all we have, with wisdom, grace, and integrity. We need courage to live with this kind of intention. We need vision to keep us from becoming apathetic and just coasting through day-to-day life.

We do not know when our end will come, just as we don't know when Christ will return. Let's take the words of Christ seriously, then. Paul echoed his sentiments when he said, "Be very careful how you live, not being like those with no understanding, but live honorably with true wisdom...Take full advantage of every day as you spend your life for his purposes" (Ephesians 5:15-16). All we have is today. Let's have the courage to live with purpose.

☐ Act of Courage

Approach your choices, relationships, and work with the awareness of what you want others to remember about you in mind.

As for Me

As for me, however, I am filled with power
by the Spirit of the Lord,
with justice and courage,
to proclaim to Jacob his rebellion
and to Israel his sin.

MICAH 3:8 CSB

The Spirit of God fills us with power to walk in the mercy and light of Christ. We are empowered in grace to choose his ways. We are covered in forgiveness, taking away the weight of our sins. We are filled with passion to pursue justice and to promote peace. In all things, let us look to the Spirit of God for strength first and continuously.

Sometimes the Spirit of God gives us boldness to confront the injustices that people perpetrate. We must not turn away for fear of confrontation when the Spirit rises within us on behalf of his justice and might. Let's not be afraid to speak the truth. We can do that in love. We can call out oppressive and abusive behaviors without fear, for God is always on the side of truth and justice!

☐ Act of Courage

Have an honest conversation with those you love;
a hard one even, if you've been putting it off.

Courage to Follow

They answered Joshua, saying, "All that you have commanded us we will do, and wherever you send us we will go. Just as we obeyed Moses in all things, so we will obey you; only may the LORD your God be with you as He was with Moses."

JOSHUA 1:16-17 NASB

It can take courage to choose to trust and follow a new leader. When Moses reached the end of his life the people already were familiar with Joshua. He was no stranger to them, but he was nervous to take the place of leader over Israel. God promised to be with him, and now the people were promising to follow him just as they had followed Moses. That must have been a weight off of Joshua's chest!

This is not an encouragement to blindly follow whichever leader claims to have God's favor. That is actually quite foolish. Joshua was known by these people, which means both his strengths and his weaknesses were familiar. It takes courage to trust leadership, so choose wisely whom you will follow!

☐ Act of Courage

Get to know people, their backgrounds, and not just their own accounts of it. Know the discernment of others before jumping behind a new leader.

Only Wise Judge

There is only one true Lawgiver and Judge, the One
who has the power to save and destroy—so who do you
think you are to judge your neighbor?

JAMES 4:12 TPT

The law of love Jesus set in place leaves no room for the
judgment of others. Judgment is different from concern,
and it is more aggressive and fracturing than confrontation.
When we judge others, we assume we know their
motivations, their abilities, and their inner world. We do
not. It is not our job to criticize and judge each other. We
can only control our own actions and choices. Let's focus
on that instead, knowing we all fall short of the perfection
of God in our own way.

Jesus said, "Refuse to be a critic full of bias toward
others, and judgment will not be passed on you. For you'll
be judged by the same standard that you've used to
judge others" (Matthew 7:1-2). Keep that in mind in your
thoughts, interactions, and biases toward others today.
Choose love and grace, for in so doing, you will receive
love and grace.

❏ *Act of Courage*

*Choose to not be overly critical of others even if
those around you have made a habit of it.*

Vessels of the Spirit

"I will pour out my Spirit on all humanity;
then your sons and your daughters will prophesy,
your old men will have dreams,
and your young men will see visions."

JOEL 2:28 CSB

The Spirit of God has already been poured out in the earth.
Everyone who comes to Christ is given the Holy Spirit. This
very verse from Joel was used to describe the Pentecost in
the second chapter of Acts. We are still in these last days
when God is pouring out his Spirit. Some of us will dream
prophetic dreams, others will see visions, and still others
will prophesy.

Do you long to partake in the gifts of the Spirit? Seek him,
and you will find him. Yield the leadership of your life to
him, and he will guide you. Open up your heart to him,
and you will be filled. The children of God are the vessels
of his Spirit, and his family is large and ever expanding. As
Peter said, all those who long for him must, "Repent and be
baptized…in the name of Jesus Christ for the forgiveness
of your sins, and you will receive the gift of the Holy Spirit"
(Acts 2:38).

☐ Act of Courage

*If you haven't already, ask for the gift of
the Holy Spirit and wait upon him.*

Importance of Impact

Do not merely look out for your own personal interests,
but also for the interests of others.

PHILIPPIANS 2:4 NASB

There is no room for selfishness in the kingdom of God.
That is not to say there isn't any room for *self*. Selfishness
means to have concern for oneself to a fault. Knowing
what is healthy for us, having appropriate boundaries, and
knowing our giftings and weaknesses are an important
part of preserving our energy. There is nothing wrong with
personal interests. It is when we are *only* concerned with
our own interests that selfishness takes over.

The kingdom of God is always expanding, reaching out,
and extending mercy. It is countercultural to choose to look
out for the interests of others knowing the favor may never
be returned. But it is very like the kingdom of God to do
this! Let's love, therefore, in word and deed, in intention,
and in action. Our choices impact others whether we
recognize it or not, so let's be more intentional about the
benefit of others.

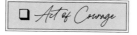

☐ *Act of Courage*

*In your interactions today consider others before
you interject your own preferences.*

Truth Abides

You yourself must be an example to them by doing good works of every kind. Let everything you do reflect the integrity and seriousness of your teaching. Teach the truth so that your teaching can't be criticized. Then those who oppose us will be ashamed and have nothing bad to say about us.

TITUS 2:7-8 NLT

Do you ever consider that your life is an example to those who know you? Only you can do anything about whether or not you present a good or a poor standard in showing submission to Christ. Do all your good works with integrity and take your work seriously. Be a person of truth when walking in the light of Christ's example. Point to him in all you do with a life that promotes peace, mercy, and grace.

Integrity can be described in many ways, but it can pretty much be summed up in this: practice what you preach. Live out what you say is important to you. Let your values match your practices. With your words and actions matching up, others know what to expect of you. Let the mercy of Christ refine you as you submit your life to his teachings.

☐ Act of Courage

Evaluate where you aren't living out what you say you want and adjust your behaviors and practices to match it.

Delighted In

The Lord your God is in your midst,
a mighty one who will save;
he will rejoice over you with gladness;
he will quiet you by his love;
he will exult over you with loud singing.

ZEPHANIAH 3:17 ESV

Do you ever feel like you are letting God down? The thing is, God knows you better than you know yourself. He is full of love for you like a caring parent is for their child. You cannot surprise or disappoint him because he already knows you through and through. Don't let your fear, shame, or guilt keep you from coming to him. He has comfort, compassion, and wisdom to shower over you as he embraces you in his loving presence.

The God who is mighty to save is the same God who rejoices wildly over his children. He loves you because he loves you, not because of what you do, how you react, or what you can offer him. Just as a parent delights in the gifts their children offer them, so God delights in your offerings. He loves you more than you can imagine.

☐ *Act of Courage*

Come to God with your disappointment, your fear, and your failures. Trust him to meet you with his incredible grace and mercy.

Celebrate the Start

"Do not despise these small beginnings,
for the Lord rejoices to see the work begin."

ZECHARIAH 4:10 NLT

Beginnings can be both exciting and daunting. They can hold an element of new possibility, but they can also feel like a far cry from the end goal. Not much that matters in life is instant. In fact, everything has a process. May we not resist the mundaneness that is required to build a life with consistency, intentionality, and practice.

Celebrate the small beginnings! As this verse states, "the Lord rejoices to see the work begin." Don't skip past the rush of excitement of a fresh start. No matter how small, it is worth being delighted over! Every step leads us closer to where we want to be if we will take it. Let's have the vision required to keep going, but let's also remember it is never too late to start again.

□ Act of Courage

Share with a close friend a small or big step you are taking and ask them to celebrate it with you!

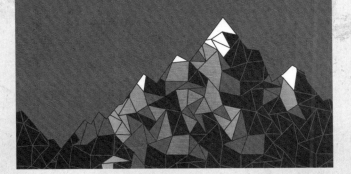

July

I can do all things through
him who strengthens me.

PHILIPPIANS 4:13 ESV

Love without Complaint

Do everything without grumbling or arguing, so that
you may become blameless and pure, "children of God
without fault in a warped and crooked generation."
Then you will shine among them like stars in the sky as
you hold firmly to the word of life.

PHILIPPIANS 2:14-15 NIV

It takes courage to own what is ours to do and to let
go of what is not our responsibility. Grumbling and
complaining, arguing and bickering happen when we
don't take responsibility for things or we feel overlooked,
manipulated, or taken for granted. Loving action does not
require reciprocation, though it certainly can hope for it.

Let's make sure today that what we do for others is a gift.
The areas that cause us to complain are questions to look
at within ourselves with curiosity before we bring them
to others. Clarity can lead to conversations laced with
kindness and compassion, all the while being open and
direct about our experiences and expectations. Love leads
the way for deeper connection, so let's practice it until it
becomes natural.

☐  Act of Courage

*Instead of arguing with someone over a task that needs
to be done, do what you can and leave the rest to a
conversation when you're not so worked up about it.*

Courage to Rebuild

I also told them how God had been kind to me and what the king had said to me. Then they answered, "Let's start rebuilding." So they began to work hard.

NEHEMIAH 2:18 NCV

When things have fallen apart, it can be devastating. When we put our efforts into building our dreams and then find they have been destroyed, delayed, or completely derailed, it is incredibly discouraging. We must take the time to grieve what has been lost; grief cannot and should not be avoided.

After a time, with close friends, family, and trusted confidants to support us, we can rebuild. We may reminisce about the way things used to be, but there is more to come. It takes a tremendous amount of courage to rebuild in hope. Let's look to the example of Jesus who is with us every step of the way. He is kind, and he will continue to be kind to us.

☐ *Act of Courage*

Take a step toward dreaming and rebuilding an area of your life that feels desolate.

Our Own Eyes

"I know that my Redeemer lives,
and he will stand upon the earth at last.
And after my body has decayed,
yet in my body I will see God! I will see him for myself.
Yes, I will see him with my own eyes.
I am overwhelmed at the thought!"

JOB 19:25-27 NLT

Job caught a glimpse of his glorious future even while grappling with his devastating grief over a great loss in his life. If Job, who was a man infamously acquainted with sorrow, could find the courage to look beyond the pain of his present circumstances into the hope that awaited him, then can't we also do the same?

Christ our Redeemer reigns in triumph, and he will stand upon the dust of the earth once more. We will each see him for ourselves and no partial glimpses or seeing only with eyes of faith will be required anymore. We will know him fully, even as we are fully known. Let us then follow Job's example and remind our souls that *we will see God face-to-face*. What a reality to look forward to!

❏ Act of Courage

Read this verse out loud over your own heart whenever you need a boost of encouragement and perspective today.

You Are His

"When you pass through the waters,
I will be with you,
and the rivers will not overwhelm you.
When you walk through the fire,
you will not be scorched,
and the flame will not burn you."

ISAIAH 43:2 CSB

Directly before the Lord spoke these words to Jacob, he said, "Do not fear, for I have redeemed you; I have called you by name, you are mine." What the Lord said to Jacob he also says to each of his children. Christ our Redeemer has freed us from the chains of sin, and we are his. We belong to him.

With that in mind, reread today's verse. The God who went before the Israelites and parted the Red Sea so they could walk across on dry land is the God who goes before you. Where you see a dead end, God sees no limit. Lean into his presence and ask for the grace to see with his perspective. Look to him for help and instruction, then follow him. The flames did not consume Daniel's friends in the furnace, and the flames of your trials will not consume you. Jesus stands with you; he is with you in the fire.

❏ *Act of Courage*

*For every challenge you encounter today,
remind yourself that God is with you. Keep going.*

Make Room

Sow for yourselves righteousness;
Reap in mercy;
Break up your fallow ground,
For it is time to seek the Lord,
Till He comes and rains righteousness on you.

Hosea 10:12 NKJV

Our character is not refined without friction. We do not grow without needing to step outside of the bounds of what we have already known. Every new stage is an opportunity to expand our understanding. May we be people who pursue righteousness, mercy, and justice. With intentionality and purpose, may we grow in compassion and honest integrity.

Every person, every life, has areas that are dormant and remain unused. When we break up the fallow ground of our lives, we till the soil of our hearts and lives to make it ready for new life. Before we sow even one seed, we need to make the soil ready. May we have the courage to make ourselves ready for new fields of life to bloom!

❑ Act of Courage

Evaluate if there is an area of your life where there hasn't been much life happening and ask the Lord to help take steps toward making it ready for revival.

Every Kindness Matters

> Do not neglect to show hospitality to strangers, for thereby some have entertained angels unawares.
>
> HEBREWS 13:2 ESV

It cannot be overstated. The teaching of Jesus points us back to the golden rule: "Do to others as you would have them do to you" (Luke 6:31 NIV). May we let love be the guiding light of our lives when we are interacting with people. We must love others as we love ourselves, making their needs as much a priority as our own are to us. Whether we are with a friend or a stranger, let's make room for the generosity of kindness to flow from our lives. When we do this, we reflect the mighty mercy of God available to each of us.

Kindness is a practice. Hospitality is something each of us can grow in. It is not intrinsic to who we are. Let's take courage in being intentional with sharing what we have with others. God is gracious and generous with us, and he gives us all we need to answer the call to share. Even the smallest act of kindness offered with loving generosity, can be a boon of encouragement to those who need it.

☐ *Act of Courage*

If offered the opportunity to help a stranger today, do it!

Rejoice Anyway

> Though the fig tree does not bud and there are no grapes on the vines, though the olive crop fails and the fields produce no food, though there are no sheep in the pen and no cattle in the stalls, yet I will rejoice in the Lord, I will be joyful in God my Savior.
>
> HABAKKUK 3:17-18 NIV

Even if your circumstances do not align with the goodness of God, even if it is hard to see in the dark of cloudy nights, can you still rejoice in the Lord? Can you choose to be joyful in God, your Savior? Isaiah 40:28 states, "The Lord is the everlasting God, the Creator of the ends of the earth. He will not grow tired or weary."

In Psalm 90, Moses is quoted as saying, "Before the mountains were born or you brought forth the whole world, from everlasting to everlasting you are God." *From everlasting to everlasting.* The Creator of all things has not changed, nor will he. He is full of mercy, justice, and truth. He is more glorious than we can fathom. Let's rejoice in who he is, for he is better than we can imagine!

☐ Act of Courage

Rejoice in the nature of God even when it is hard to see his goodness in your circumstances.

Favor of God

The LORD was with Joseph and extended kindness to him. He granted him favor with the prison warden. The warden did not bother with anything under Joseph's authority, because the LORD was with him, and the LORD made everything that he did successful.

GENESIS 39:21, 23 CSB

The amount of trust Jospeh's jailer placed in him reflects the character of the man in question. The Lord was with Joseph even in his captivity, giving him opportunities to display his trustworthiness. The favor of God was all over Joseph's story even when his brothers betrayed him. His life was spared even when some of his brothers wanted him gone for good.

May we look for the places where God's favor meets us in our own lives. What are the areas in which God has given us favor with others? May we steward their trust well, and may we live with integrity always following through on our word. May we be reliable and true without the need to show off. May we be true to who we are and who God has created us to be. There is beauty in a life lived with authenticity and honor.

☐ *Act of Courage*

Do the tasks that are yours to do, and whenever new opportunities are presented, continue to work with honesty and care.

We Are His

We're no longer living like slaves under the law, but we enjoy being God's very own sons and daughters! And because we're his, we can access everything our Father has—for we are heirs of God through Jesus, the Messiah!

GALATIANS 4:7 TPT

When you consider who God is and who you are to him, what comes up? Does he feel like a far-off figure, dictating your life like a CEO or a grandfather? Or is he like a loving parent whom you know well, who supports you, who wants what is best for you, and who offers you all he can?

May today be the day where you draw closer to the reality of God's loving-kindness toward you. He is a good, good Father, not just as the song suggests but as his character guarantees. He pursues you with passion, and he always has good intentions for you. Do you trust his heart? It is hard to trust someone you do not know well. Give time to getting to know his loving nature more today. Read through the descriptions Jesus gave of the Father. Acquaint yourself with the parables that speak of the Father's love, and let it drive your own heart to open to him.

☐ *Act of Courage*

Ask for a greater experiential revelation of God's love for you and spend time in prayer and in the Word waiting on him today.

Glorious Presence

All around him was a glowing halo, like a rainbow shining in the clouds on a rainy day. This is what the glory of the LORD looked like to me. When I saw it, I fell face down on the ground, and I heard someone's voice speaking to me.

EZEKIEL 1:28 NLT

There are a several descriptions of God's glory in the Bible. Moses was not the only one who glimpsed at it. Many prophets did. Ezekiel described his own encounter with the marvelous presence of God in this vision. It was so overwhelming that he fell face down on the ground. The presence of the Lord is powerful, and it is more magnificent than can be perfectly described.

The glory of the Lord may look different to you, but that does not mean it is any less real or life changing. The presence of God is full of brilliant light which overwhelms our senses with the radiance of his love. What Ezekiel, Moses, Peter, and others experienced, we can also experience ourselves through the Holy Spirit. May we ask for greater revelation and for dreams and visions that reveal the glory of God to us.

☐ *Act of Courage*

Ask God for a glimpse of his glory.

Alive in Christ

God, being rich in mercy, because of His great love with
which He loved us, even when we were dead in our
transgressions, made us alive together with Christ
(by grace you have been saved).

EPHESIANS 2:4-5 NASB

Even when we act like rebellious children, God's love is
undeterred. Consider the parable of the prodigal son. When
the son returned after wasting away his inheritance, how
did his father react? Did he scold or shame him? Did he turn
him away? No. He ran out to meet him when he was still a
ways off. He threw a welcome home party, covering his son
in his own robe. Even though the son was prepared to beg
for a servant's place in his father's house, the father was
overjoyed to have his son come home to him. He restored
him with love, and he celebrated his return!

This is the love of the Father that Jesus described, and it is
this same love that Paul talks about in Ephesians. We have
been saved by grace, made alive in his love. Every time we
turn to him, his love is as overwhelmingly pure as it ever was.

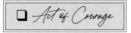

❑ *Act of Courage*

*If there is someone you have been keeping at a distance
because of hurt, consider forgiving them
and restoring the relationship.*

Rising Up

Your faith and love rise within you as you access all the treasures of your inheritance stored up in the heavenly realm. For the revelation of the true gospel is as real today as the day you first heard of our glorious hope, now that you have believed in the truth of the gospel.

COLOSSIANS 1:5 TPT

When we access the generosity of God's resources through his Spirit, faith and love rise within us. Where the Spirit of the Lord is, there is freedom. Where the Spirit of the Lord is, there are the fruits of Christ's kingdom. There is love, joy, peace, patience, kindness, gentleness, and self-control. There is grace, hope, and there is love; always love.

When was the last time you experienced faith and love rising within your heart and soul? What caused it to swell within you? As you remember, tune into that same feeling today. Tune into the hope, the grace, the promise. The same Spirit who moved within you then will move in you now, increasing your expectation and building your faith!

☐ *Act of Courage*

Remember a time when you felt hopeful, and dare to let it wash over you again, awakening to the possibility that still awaits you even if it looks different now.

Let It Flow

Let justice flow like a river,
and let goodness flow like a never-ending stream.

Amos 5:24 NCV

The flow of a river is as natural as it gets. Unless we shore it up with dams or redirect it with our intervention, rivers flow where they will. Will we allow justice to flow like a river without intervening to stop it? Will we let goodness flow like a freshwater stream straight from the Source itself?

Our lives can be conduits of the Creator's intentions, or we can work to impede it. It is more natural to surrender to love's plans than it is to build barriers. Yet how very human it is to try to control what was never ours to dictate. Let's find ourselves on the side of justice, mercy, and loving-kindness. Song of Solomon 8:7 says, "Even much water cannot put out the flame of love; floods cannot drown love." Love will always endure, so let's build our lives upon it!

❏ *Act of Courage*

Surrender to God's love today and let it compel you in justice, goodness, and mercy-kindness.

Continuous Devotion

They were continually devoting themselves
to the apostles' teaching and to fellowship,
to the breaking of bread and to prayer.

ACTS 2:42 NASB

Devotion is no small thing. It takes concerted effort
and intentionality to be devoted to something. It is
not an afterthought, but rather, it's an important value.
What are you devoted to? What fills your time and your
relationships? Who or what do you spend your time on?
What is your attention drawn to or fixated on over and
over again?

We may just find we are devoted to things that don't
actually add value to our lives. Where our energy goes,
there is our devotion. May we choose the things we want
to invest in and follow through with our attention, our time,
and our resources. If our family is a priority, then we will
make sacrifices elsewhere. If we are devoted to fellowship
and praying together, we must also make sacrifices. May
we have the courage to put what truly matters first, and to
continue to devote ourselves to love, faith, and peace.

☐ *Act of Courage*

*Decide what areas you need to cut down on
in order to make room for the important things,
and to take steps toward that today.*

Always Worth It

Never become tired of doing good.

2 Thessalonians 3:13 NCV

Doing the right thing is always a good choice. This is as true for making an honest living as it is for treating others with care and compassion. Our whole lives can be an expression of worship to the Lord. Our work, too, can be an offering to the Lord, no matter what kind of work it is. When we abide by the laws of the land and seek to enrich the lives of others through doing the right thing with integrity, we walk in the light of truth.

Every type of work is important work. Grocery store workers are as important as business owners. Don't get so caught up in the type of work you do that you forget that all things done with integrity matter. Have your ambitions, sure, but it is enough to do the work that is yours today no matter how menial it may seem to you.

☐  Act of Courage

Let your job be an act of offering worship to the Lord today. He sees what others overlook!

Wholehearted Surrender

Neither before nor after Josiah was there a king like him who turned to the Lord as he did—with all his heart and with all his soul and with all his strength, in accordance with all the Law of Moses.

2 KINGS 23:25 NIV

This verse is such a beautiful representation of our individuality before God. We know that King David was known as *a man after God's own heart*. Abraham was called *a friend of God*. Moses was sent by God to deliver God's people from their captivity. These are only a few examples of people who had close relationships with the Lord.

The Law of Moses which Jesus quoted when asked what he considered the most important commandment, is to "Love the Lord your God with all your heart and with all your soul and with all your mind and with all your strength" (Mark 12:30). This is what Josiah was known for, and this is what we are called to as well. May we seek to love the Lord in word, deed, and thought!

☐ *Act of Courage*

Turn to the Lord with whatever is weighing you down today and love the Lord with an open heart of surrender.

No Need to Pretend

Never once did we try to win you with flattery, as you well know. And God is our witness that we were not pretending to be your friends just to get your money. As for human praise, we have never sought it from you or anyone else.

1 THESSALONIANS 2:5-6 NLT

This verse can be summed up this way: Paul and his fellow missionaries had no hidden motives, nor did they manipulate the trust of the Thessalonian Christians in order to take advantage of them. For us, there is a grounded simplicity in being who we are honestly and openly. We do not love others with hidden agendas, or at least we shouldn't. God loves us because he loves us, not because of what we can offer him.

Let's be sure to check our hearts in our relationships. Are there hidden motivations in getting to know others or to gain their trust? Or do we truly want to love others because they are worthy of being known and loved? Each of us has inherent dignity and worth because we are created in God's image. May we live with open hearts with no need to pretend.

☐ Act of Courage

Be true to who you are and let your interactions with others be rooted in the confidence of God's love over you.

Keep Learning

Let no one deceive himself.
If anyone among you thinks that he is wise in this age,
let him become a fool that he may become wise.

1 Corinthians 3:18 ESV

No one likes a know-it-all. Think of it. Do you know anyone who can never admit when they're wrong? It can be off-putting to be around someone who uses pride as a constant shield and measure. The way of the kingdom of Christ is different from the ways of this world. We must remain teachable, admitting that there is so much more we don't know than we do know.

It is a strength to be open to changing our minds. It is a powerful person who can admit they were wrong and change course when they know better. May we not resist the refining process of expanding our knowledge, especially as we grow deeper in our faith and more varied in our experience. A fool for God, trusting his leadership and transforming under his correction, is a vessel of his wisdom.

☐ Act of Courage

Be open about your growth with others as you discover areas where you didn't see the whole picture. Admit to being wrong when you are.

Every Opportunity

Whenever we have the opportunity, we should do good to everyone—especially to those in the family of faith.

GALATIANS 6:10 NLT

What would it look like for those who follow Jesus to try to outdo one another in love? There would be incredible encouragement, needs would be met, and hospitality would overflow in these communities. Generosity of heart, of resources, and of time would be a priority played out in relationships. People would feel seen, known, and loved.

Even if this kind of community sounds like a foreign concept as we consider our own experiences within Christianity, may we strive to be those who love each other well. Let's do good to everyone whenever we have the opportunity. Instead of distancing ourselves from the needs of others, let's look for ways we can share love in practical measures. Instead of overly focusing on what is not going right, let's look at ways we can make a difference in our own spheres. Every day is filled with opportunities to practice kindness in action. Let's be intentional with compassion, reliability, and generosity today!

❑ Act of Courage

Instead of rushing through your day, look for opportunities to slow down and connect with others.

New Growth

"I am doing something brand new, something unheard of. Even now it sprouts and grows and matures. Don't you perceive it? I will make a way in the wilderness and open up flowing streams in the desert."

ISAIAH 43:19 TPT

Even as each new day is a little bit different from the last, every moment is an opportunity to look for where God is sowing new mercies. Within the rhythm of the seasons there is an ebb and flow, and yet every year is distinct. Last winter was not the same as the one before, and this summer holds different opportunities, both within nature and in our lives, than last summer did.

Will we have the courage to look beyond the decay of broken dreams to the new life that sprouts from the soil of our lives? God is always up to something new. He always sows life even in the most devastating areas of our lives. May we look for where the light shines on the sprouts of new growth. The most desolate of areas can produce fruit that is surprisingly beautiful.

☐ *Act of Courage*

Ask the Lord for eyes to see where he is doing something brand new in your life.

Led in Triumph

Thanks be to God, who always leads us in triumph in Christ, and through us reveals the fragrance of the knowledge of Him in every place.

2 Corinthians 2:14 NASB

This passage of Scripture continues by saying, "We are a fragrance of Christ to God among those who are being saved and among those who are perishing." To one, we are the aroma of life and to the other, the aroma of death. What does this actually mean? Through our yielded lives Christ is displayed, and it is the unmistakable fragrance of the victory of the Redeemer.

For those who yield their lives to Christ, they recognize the aroma of Christ's resurrection life through us. For those who resist his ways, living according to his mercy, justice, and peace, it is unappealing altogether. No matter what others think of us, let's remain submitted to the kingdom values of Christ, for through his life we are led in triumph from glory to glory!

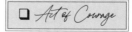

☐ Act of Courage

Don't worry what others will think about your choices; make each one according to God's leadership in your life. You can always trust him.

A Humble Heart

The humble of heart will inherit every promise
and enjoy abundant peace.

PSALM 37:11 TPT

Jesus said in Matthew 5:5 that the meek will inherit the earth. It is with gentleness, kindness, and flexibility we enjoy the incredible peace of God. Every promise of God is fulfilled in *him*. We can come to him with confidence, knowing we will find all we are looking for. The longings and needs we have are fulfilled in his Being.

Let's learn to loosen our grasp on what we consider ours, or our right to have. Let's live with the understanding that what we have is a gift, and our security is not in how much we own. Living for God means following his ways, being fueled by his love, and resting in his faithfulness. Let's build our lives upon the firm foundation of his mercy, not becoming overly confident in our creature comforts.

❏ *Act of Courage*

Be intentionally generous with what you have today. Share what you don't normally share. Let go of the incessant need for instant gratification. Instead, choose to wait on what you feel you must have. Give it time and space to breathe so you don't act on impulse but create space for peace.

Immeasurable Power

> To him who is able to do above and beyond all that we ask or think according to the power that works in us.
>
> EPHESIANS 3:20 CSB

The power of God is not only displayed in Christ's resurrection from the dead. It is not only found in miracles that leave us breathless and in awe. Those are incredible instances, to be sure, and God does move in miraculous ways today through his Spirit. There is also an inner transformation that God's power works within us, beyond what others can see or recognize.

The God who is full of extravagant love pours over us until we overflow with his fullness. In this spiritual flooding, our souls are refreshed, our perspectives have shifted, and our understanding is expanded. What a marvelous mystery! Let's invite the power of God's love to move through us, not only in meeting physical needs, but also the deep emotional ones that we don't even know how to express.

☐ Act of Courage

Ask God to shift a perspective, heal a heartbreak, or comfort a loss that sits deeply within you.

Divine Words

"When you are arrested, don't worry about how to respond or what to say. God will give you the right words at the right time. For it is not you who will be speaking—it will be the Spirit of your Father speaking through you."

MATTHEW 10:19-20 NLT

Sometimes anxiety keeps us from staying rooted in the present. One of the ways anxiety can show up in our systems is by overthinking potential situations that may occur in the future. The problem with this is there is no limit to what *might* happen, so our brains don't take a break from the possible threats that await us. But the peace of God is always available in Christ to calm our minds and settle our hearts.

We know God is with us. He's not surprised by anything that may startle us, and he is full of wisdom. If we know this to be true, if we have faith in his loyal nature and his reliable leadership, then we can rest in trusting he will help us right when we need it.

☐ Act of Courage

When you feel your mind jumping ahead with anxiety, ask the Holy Spirit to fill you with peace, take a deep breath, and ground yourself in the moment.

Interceding for Us

Who can say God's people are guilty? No one, because
Christ Jesus died, but he was also raised from the dead,
and now he is on God's right side, appealing to God for us.

ROMANS 8:34 NCV

If Christ will not condemn us, who will? He is the one who
gave his life for us. He conquered death, tearing the veil
that separated God's holy presence from the people and
opening the divide that stood between us. There is now
nothing that separates us from God's love!

Jesus sits at the right hand of his Father interceding for
us and praying for our triumph. Consider the implications
of this. Jesus is actively engaged in talking to the Father
about us for our good and for our victory. May we live
today with the confidence of God's help knowing we are
not alone. May we be bold with the knowledge God is
listening not only to our prayers but also to the prayers
that Jesus prays for us!

☐ *Act of Courage*

*Refuse to let shame or guilt keep you trapped in cycles
from which Christ has already freed you!*

Comfort and Compassion

Sing for joy, O heavens, and exult, O earth;
break forth, O mountains, into singing!
For the LORD has comforted his people
and will have compassion on his afflicted.

ISAIAH 49:13 ESV

Even though we are not promised a pain-free life, it does not mean that God is not good. He is our close Comforter in our time of heartbreak and loss. He has incredible compassion on our hurts. He does not demand what we cannot give. We are not workhorses in his kingdom. We are his children, and he loves us through and through.

It is backwards to demand joy when one is suffering. It is through the relief of comfort one can rejoice. Pain is not a sin, and suffering is not a sign of failure. It is human, and Jesus experienced the depths of it himself. Instead of trying to escape our pain, let's invite the Holy Spirit to come close and comfort us. Let's turn to him and receive his compassion.

☐ Act of Courage

Instead of trying to escape hard feelings when they come up today, invite God to meet you and minister to you in them.

Trust the Timing

Do not forget this one thing, dear friends:
With the Lord a day is like a thousand years,
and a thousand years are like a day.

2 PETER 3:8 NIV

When your patience is running thin, and you feel as if you are ready to give up hope remember all is not lost. God's timing is not your own. Proverbs 13:12 describes the struggle with timing well, "Hope deferred makes the heart sick, but a longing fulfilled is a tree of life." The God who is loyal in love to all that he has made has not forgotten you even if you are heartsick in the waiting.

Deuteronomy 7:9 reminds us to rely on the faithfulness of God: "Know therefore that the Lord your God is God; he is the faithful God, keeping his covenant of love to a thousand generations of those who love him and keep his commandments." Love the Lord your God, love others, and trust his timing. He will come through for you!

☐ *Act of Courage*

Let go of the need to control the timing or outcome of things that are out of your hands! Trust God, for he will not fail you.

Greater Than

This is the way we know that we belong to the way of truth. When our hearts make us feel guilty, we can still have peace before God. God is greater than our hearts, and he knows everything. My dear friends, if our hearts do not make us feel guilty, we can come without fear into God's presence.

1 John 3:19-21 NCV

There are times when our thoughts lead us down paths that stir up guilt over what we could have done better in the past. Though we cannot change the past, we can receive grace to forgive ourselves just as God in Christ has forgiven us. What God does not hold against us, we can let go of.

Is there an area of your life where you struggle with guilt, something you wish you could change? Ask the Lord for his peace to wash over you and the grace to forgive yourself for not knowing or doing better at the time. The power of God transforms you to choose better now and to walk without fear into the glorious presence of the Lord who leads you in loving-kindness!

☐ Act of Courage

When you feel guilt, shame, or disappointment over things you cannot change, remind yourself you are already forgiven and free in the eyes of God, and you don't have to punish yourself any longer.

Courage to Grow

Leaving the elementary teaching about the Christ, let us press on to maturity, not laying again a foundation of repentance from dead works and of faith toward God, of instruction about washings and laying on of hands, and the resurrection of the dead and eternal judgment.

HEBREWS 6:1-2 NASB

It takes courage to move on from places of comfort into challenging new areas. This is true when growing up and leaving the house, and this is true when growing in our faith. The foundations of our faith are building blocks for the future. As we grow in maturity, we cannot remain in the same spaces of simple understanding that no longer serve to teach us more than we already know.

Children need the protection of their parents and the guidance of their community to help them build foundations of growth. But once the children have grown, they each get to make their own choices and experience the freedom of building a life that is their own. Are we afraid to let people do this in their relationships with Christ, or do we recognize that this too, is a necessary step in spiritual maturity?

☐ Act of Courage

Look for ways to expand your faith in broader ways as you grow in Christ.

Refreshing Generosity

The generous soul will be made rich,
And he who waters will also be watered himself.

PROVERBS 11:25 NKJV

Generosity makes room for us to receive. When we freely share what we have with others, we help cover needs as well as open up more space in our lives. A vessel in God's kingdom that actively pours out to others is able to be refilled by the gracious abundance of God's love. When we run dry, he fills our cup.

Instead of hoarding what we have in the case of what-ifs, let's be generous. This is not to say that we should forsake wise planning. When we prepare with discerning strategies, we are more equipped to share out of excess rather than scrambling to help others when we are, ourselves, depleted. Generosity does not forsake wisdom, nor does wisdom overlook generosity. Let's take each in our grip as we look ahead!

☐ *Act of Courage*

Share what you have with those who have less than you do today. Be specific and give it without expecting anything in return.

Nothing Is Hidden

There is no such thing as darkness with you.
The night, to you, is as bright as the day;
there's no difference between the two.

PSALM 139:12 TPT

Have you ever been afraid of the dark? Perhaps your imagination runs wild when shadows form on the walls, or the normal creaks of a house seem eerie in the still of the night. Maybe the dark doesn't bother you at all, but the unknowns of your future keep you up at night. Whatever it is that feels like darkness to you—that which is shadowy, unclear, and mysterious—know it is perfectly clear to the Lord.

Trust God with what you don't know, and let his nearness, his strength, and his wisdom uphold you. Nothing is hidden from him. Not a detail goes overlooked. He is not worried, so throw all your worries at him! Let him take them. He can hold the space for them and give your heart rest. May you find peace in his faithful care today.

☐ *Act of Courage*

**When you are afraid of what you cannot see,
remind your heart that nothing is hidden from God.**

August

"Don't worry, because I am with you.
Don't be afraid, because I am your God.
I will make you strong and will help you;
I will support you with my right hand
that saves you."

ISAIAH 41:10 NCV

The Honorable Path

Never pay back evil with more evil. Do things in such a way that everyone can see you are honorable.

ROMANS 12:17 NLT

In a world where people applaud the clapback, it takes courage to choose the higher path. Our natural inclination is to return evil with evil, to return insult with insult, punch with punch, and humiliation with disgrace. What kind of perspective or self-control would it take to choose the honorable return? What if we offered a blessing for a curse and gracious patience for another's irritation?

We cannot control how others will act toward us, but we can influence our own choices. We get to choose how we will live, how we will treat others, and how we will respond. Let's take Paul's advice and do things in a such a way everyone can see we are honorable. When we let go of our grudges and the need to get even, we get to put our energy to better use.

☐ Act of Courage

Think through how you want to respond to others today, and every time you feel your defenses going up, choose what you want rather than what is natural.

Important Reminders

Remind them to submit to rulers and authorities, to obey, to be ready for every good work, to slander no one, to avoid fighting, and to be kind, always showing gentleness to all people.

TITUS 3:1-2 CSB

As Christians, we don't get to ignore our civic duty to society. We are not outside the law, nor should we take liberties we would not expect others to abide by. As followers of Christ, there is no excuse for tearing others down with our words no matter who they are! Much has been said and done in the name of Christ that does not represent his character at all. May we be careful not to follow the example of hotheaded people. May we be pursuers of peace at every level.

Choosing to follow the loving way of Christ means we must lay down our rights to being right. No argument is worth it if it builds walls between us, separating us into categories that are built by our own fears, judgments, and need for certainty. Let's instead be considerate and humble to everyone!

☐ *Act of Courage*

Refuse to engage in an argument that has no chance for resolution.

Courage to Confess

> Look and listen carefully. Hear the prayer that I, your servant, am praying to you day and night for your servants, the Israelites. I confess the sins we Israelites have done against you. My father's family and I have sinned against you.
>
> NEHEMIAH 1:6 NCV

It takes a real honest look at ourselves as well as some humility to admit when we have messed up. We can't hide anything from God, and chances are we aren't fooling anyone else either. Let's have the courage to be real about our failures, both big and small. We are all human, and we all fall short of the glory of God. In short, we are human, and we can't be perfect.

Let's give up the façade, the need to appear put together in every area of our lives. None of us has it all together. Not one. Perfectionism is a trap, and it keeps us from living in the gracious tension of our humanness. Let's not hide from our sins but confess them. When we bring them into the light, Christ's forgiveness covers us.

☐ Act of Courage

*Be bold. Admit when you are wrong,
where you've gotten things offtrack and
ask for forgiveness from those it affected.*

There Is Room

"Let not your heart be troubled; you believe in God, believe also in Me. In My Father's house are many mansions. I go to prepare a place for you. And if I go and prepare a place for you, I will come again and receive you to Myself; that where I am, there you may be also."

JOHN 14:1-3 NKJV

The kingdom of God is not exclusive. There is no shortage of rooms in the Father's house. He welcomes all who come to him. Every person is made in the image of Love. Let's never forget that. No one is left out of the open invitation of God's kingdom. We are all called to take our places as his children, being loved and loving others in the same generous way.

Have you ever felt like you disqualified yourself from God's love? It isn't possible! Every time you come to him, he meets you with the magnitude of his mercy and his unending loving-kindness. You cannot exhaust his compassion no matter how hard you try. Take courage in the truth that Christ has prepared a specific place for you in his Father's kingdom.

❏ *Act of Courage*

Refuse to put limits on God's love for yourself and for others as you go about your day.

Call and Answer

"Call to me and I will answer you, and will tell you great and hidden things that you have not known."

JEREMIAH 33:3 ESV

How gracious is it that when we call to God, he answers? Not only does he answer us by reminding us of what we already know, but he reveals new things to us. There is so much to discover in the wisdom of God. There is no end to the marvelous mysteries of his kingdom, and we see that with each new revelation. Consequently, we hunger for more!

May today be the day you call on the Lord no matter where you are or what you are doing. Open a line of communication, a conversation that keeps going throughout the day. The Holy Spirit is near and can reveal the hidden things of God's heart as you listen! May you know the wonderful joy of the liberating wisdom of God breaking open your understanding and giving you fresh revelation of his indescribable goodness.

☐ *Act of Courage*

Pray continually throughout the day even if you never speak a word out loud.

Not Even a Shadow

Whatever is good and perfect is a gift coming down to us from God our Father, who created all the lights in the heavens. He never changes or casts a shifting shadow.

JAMES 1:17 NLT

Have you ever thought about the line from the hymn, Great is Thy Faithfulness, which says, "There is no shadow of turning with Thee?" It is easy to sing something without putting thought into the meaning behind it. I remember when I realized the significance of this phrase. There is no shadow of turning with God because he never turns to leave. He is steadfast, unmoved. He is faithful, and he never abandons us!

God never changes or casts a shifting shadow, not even a slight shift. What a beautiful truth to hold onto today and every day. Whatever situations you are facing, whatever fears or shame you are battling within yourself, the love of God burns bright and close. He will not leave you. He will not abandon you in your pain. He will not turn you away when you come to him, and he is never too busy to take time for you.

❏ Act of Courage

Instead of running from pain when you see it in others, consider staying and loving them through it.

Do It Again

Do it again!
Those Yahweh has set free will return to Zion
and come celebrating with songs of joy!
They will be crowned with never-ending joy!
Gladness and joy will overwhelm them;
despair and depression will disappear!

ISAIAH 51:11 TPT

It takes courage to not give up when things get hard. It takes courage to not lose hope. What the Lord has done before, he will do again. He brings relief, comfort, and restoration. He redeems what we lost and brings new life out of the ashes. We are free in the love of Christ, free to experience his joy, gladness, and peace. We are free to look forward to the goodness ahead and free to celebrate new beginnings. Free!

Let's make this our prayer: "Do it again, Lord!" Do it again. Bring healing, bring joy, and bring hope. Bring us the abundant life of your Spirit, breaking down the barriers that keep us from experiencing the fullness of your life within us. Bring us the pure love of your presence. Bring us all we need, and all we long for!

☐ Act of Courage

Write your own prayer. Be as poetic or artistic as you want starting with, "Do it again!"

Magnificent Sunrise

"Let us acknowledge the LORD;
let us press on to acknowledge him.
As surely as the sun rises,
he will appear;
he will come to us like the winter rains,
like the spring rains that water the earth."

HOSEA 6:3 NIV

Sometimes our waning hope can be lifted by turning our attention to the truth. Nature expresses many of the attributes of God; sunrises, sunsets, and seasons, to name a few. The glory of God is hidden in the world around us. Music connects our souls to the atmosphere, changing us through the sound waves that penetrate our bodies. Poetic language and artistic expression speak to our hearts and minds all at once. Every sense can be used to experience the beauty of the Lord.

Let us acknowledge the Lord in our hearing and in our sight. Let's press on to acknowledge him through the sensation of touch and taste. Let's thank him for the aromas that reflect hunger, sweetness, and satisfaction. Let's offer our worship through each of our senses today!

☐ Act of Courage

*Tune in to each sense as you spend time with the Lord today.
Thank him for the ability to experience him in these ways.*

God Can Use Anything

*As for you, you meant evil against me, but God meant it
for good in order to bring about this present result, to
keep many people alive.*

GENESIS 50:20 NASB

Even what others mean to harm us, God can turn around
and use for good. He cannot be fooled, and he is skilled
at bringing restoration to what seems irreparable. Joseph
was sold by his brothers into slavery. What a cruel thing to
do! And yet, this was not the end of Joseph's story but the
beginning of God's work of favor in his life.

Joseph had many years to forgive his brothers before he
faced them again. In that time, he had gone through many
challenges, but he also was trusted with great leadership.
He ended up working for Pharaoh in a high position. His
brothers were ashamed and fearful when they saw him, but
Joseph forgave them. Not only that, but he took care of
them! May we have humble hearts which are able to forgive
those who harm us, knowing God will use even what was
meant to harm us, for good.

❏ *Act of Courage*

*Ask God to redeem the things that seem
irredeemable in your past.*

Strength in Partnership

Two people are better than one, because they get more
done by working together. If one falls down, the other
can help him up. But it is bad for the person who is
alone and falls, because no one is there to help.

ECCLESIASTES 4:9-10 NCV

It is not a virtue to go it alone in life. There is strength in
support and knowing you have someone to count on. You
can offer each other encouragement as you build toward a
shared goal. Though one person may be easily swayed, the
council of two is harder to manipulate.

May we be willing to take the risk of vulnerability, the work
of partnership, and the humility necessary for both with
those who are important in our lives. Let's not give up on
the significance others can have in our lives. Not everyone
is worthy of our trust, but there are those that are! May we
have the discernment to choose our partners well in love,
friendship, and business.

☐ Act of Courage

*Ask for help doing something you have been
putting off doing on your own.*

Transformed by Glory

We all, with unveiled faces, are looking as in a mirror at the glory of the Lord and are being transformed into the same image from glory to glory; this is from the Lord who is the Spirit.

2 CORINTHIANS 3:18 CSB

The glory of the Lord is not saved for some; it is for all who look to God. It "comes from the Lord, the Spirit," as the verse states above. All of us are transformed as we look to the Lord. Our transformations are unique, but the fruit of them is what the Spirit produces in us. Love, joy, peace, patience, and kindness are universally the work of the Spirit.

As we go "from one degree of glory to another," as Paul puts it, we develop into different versions of who we were always created to be. We constantly evolve as people. Think back to who you were five years ago. Can you honestly say nothing has changed? Chances are you have different interests, a more developed style, and think differently than you did about some subjects. As we submit to Christ, how we change reflects his kingdom values. Let's continue to live under his leadership!

Act of Courage

Consider where you have grown in life and allow others the space to change in their own ways and timing, trusting them to God.

Mindful in Suffering

This is a gracious thing, when, mindful of God,
one endures sorrows while suffering unjustly.

1 PETER 2:19 ESV

No one likes to suffer. Though some of us are more acquainted with suffering than others, it does not mean any of us can escape it. Peter echoed Jesus' teachings when he said it "is a gracious thing, when one endures sorrows while suffering unjustly." Jesus put it this way: "Blessed are those who are persecuted for righteousness' sake" (Matthew 5:10). Even in our suffering, we are surrounded by grace.

May we dare look at the unjust suffering, the pain we never caused nor asked for, in our lives with fresh eyes today. We are not being punished, least of all by God. Suffering is not an indictment of sin. It is a part of the human experience. When we accept that we cannot change whether we will suffer or not, we can redirect our focus when we are in the midst of it. And here's where we can move our attention: God with us. His gracious presence in us, to comfort, strengthen, and heal.

☐ *Act of Courage*

When you feel the unfairness of your suffering, recognize you are not alone in it. God is with you, and everyone around you also suffers in some way. You are truly not alone.

Beneficial in Every Way

Bodily exercise profits a little, but godliness is profitable for all things, having promise of the life that now is and of that which is to come.

1 TIMOTHY 4:8 NKJV

How many of us look at athletes and think, "Wow, what discipline they must have!" We can see the effects of their efforts on their bodies and how they move. They can do what untrained people cannot. It is the same with spiritual discipline and strengthening. It may be harder to spot on the outside, but it is just as recognizable under the right conditions, for example, if someone is under any type of pressure!

Let's train our spirits, our minds, and our hearts in godliness. It takes as much intention and follow-through as training our bodies requires. But small changes build bigger ones. Don't read this as saying you need an overhaul of your life. You don't need to restrict everything. Start by identifying your values and take one small step each day to grow one of them. As you add the things that add value to your life, it is much easier to sacrifice the things that don't. Small steps with consistency take you far!

☐ *Act of Courage*

Choose one thing you can do each day to grow your spiritual strength.

A Time Like This

"If you keep quiet at a time like this, deliverance and relief for the Jews will arise from some other place, but you and your relatives will die. Who knows if perhaps you were made queen for just such a time as this?"

ESTHER 4:14 NLT

There was a lot of pressure on Esther to use her favor with the king to intervene for her people. His right-hand man was scheming to kill the Jewish people. Though Haman, the man who plotted this, did not know Esther was a Jew, she still did not know if the king would believe her over his trusted confidant. She risked her own life to try to save her people. And yet, what other choice did she have?

There may be a situation that feels too risky for you to speak the truth. Perhaps it is at work or with friends. Maybe it is in a church setting. You probably aren't facing the possibility of death, but of disconnection, ruptured relationships, or putting your advancement on the line. Speaking the truth is incredibly important. When faced with a challenge to either protect yourself by staying quiet or helping others by speaking up, consider Mordecai's challenge to Esther: "Who knows if perhaps you were made...for just such a time as this?"

☐ Act of Courage

Choose to speak up for others.

Compelled by Compassion

The king's daughter opened the basket and saw the
baby boy. He was crying, so she felt sorry for him and
said, "This is one of the Hebrew babies."

EXODUS 2:6 NCV

Even though Pharaoh had ordered all of the Hebrew boys
be killed, his daughter found Moses in a basket sent down
the river. Instantly, she recognized he was a Hebrew baby,
but she did not follow the orders of her father and hand
him over. Instead, she was compelled by compassion to
care for him as her own son. And that's what she did!

Has compassion ever moved you to break the rules? There
is a difference between knowing what is expected and
what is right. May you always err on the side of love, the
kind of love that protects lives, cares for the vulnerable,
and makes sacrifices in order to do so. You may just find
you are the answer to someone else's prayer for help.

☐ Act of Courage

*When faced with a choice that costs you something,
choose the option that is the most loving!*

When You Don't Know

By faith Abraham, when called to go to a place he
would later receive as his inheritance, obeyed and went,
even though he did not know where he was going.

HEBREWS 11:8 NIV

When God called Abraham to leave the land of his father,
the land of his comfort, he did not give him a step-by-step
plan. He didn't draw a blueprint of what each phase would
look like. Abraham did not even know where he would end
up. Still, he followed the Lord. He chose, even in ambiguity,
to obey God.

If you feel pulled in a direction that leads you out of your
comfort zone, know you are in good company. By faith,
Abraham obeyed and went. By faith, you can also follow
the Lord's leading in your life. With his promises as fuel
for your hope, trust that he will guide you every step of
the way. Don't wait until everything is clear, for an object
in motion is easy to redirect. Trust the Lord's leading. He
won't let you down.

☐ Act of Courage

*Take the step of faith you have been putting off because
you don't feel ready enough. Today is the day. Seize it.*

Even in Doubt

The LORD said to Abraham, "Why did Sarah laugh, saying, 'Shall I actually give birth to a child, when I am so old?' Is anything too difficult for the LORD? At the appointed time I will return to you, at this time next year, and Sarah will have a son."

GENESIS 18:13-14 NASB

The thing I love about this passage is that Sarah laughed. It's so incredibly human. She thought to herself, "Yeah right! My womb is dusty. There's no way I'm having a baby!" She didn't conceive in her younger years. The thought of all of a sudden becoming pregnant was so outlandish it was laughable.

And yet, we know the rest of the story. Sarah did have that baby at the ripe old age of ninety. Even though she laughed at the thought and didn't believe it possible, God did not pull back the promise. He didn't say, "Oh ye of little faith, now you don't get a baby." He made it clear anything is possible with him, and he fulfilled their long-awaited hopes. What an incredibly good God he is!

☐ *Act of Courage*

Don't give up on the long-awaited promises God has given you.

Real Relationship

The LORD said to Moses, "This very thing that you have spoken I will do, for you have found favor in my sight, and I know you by name." Moses said, "Please show me your glory."

EXODUS 33:17-18 ESV

This interaction between the Lord and Moses feels so intimate, like close friends having a heart-to-heart. The Lord longs for us to know his goodness personally. He always intended for us to have a relationship with him. He didn't create Adam and Eve to be distant figures who kind of represented him in this world that he made. He created them as friends, to be his friends. He walked with them in the garden, and he also longs to walk with us as freely right where we are.

May you take hope in the invitation the Lord offers you. Spoiler: it's an open invitation, so it doesn't expire. Spend time walking and talking with him. And then ask him your questions. Ask him to reveal himself to you. The give and take of conversation is yours through the Spirit.

☐ *Act of Courage*

Talk to God like you would your closest friend.
Don't hold anything back.

Inescapable Love

Can anything separate us from the love Christ has for us? Can troubles or problems or sufferings or hunger or nakedness or danger or violent death?

ROMANS 8:35 NCV

Romans 8 continues by saying, "But in all these things we are completely victorious through God who showed his love for us" (verse 37). Troubles, problems, or suffering can't stop God's love from reaching us. Hunger or homelessness cannot keep us from the love that covers us. When nothing else holds us, God's love does.

No matter the challenges you are facing, and no matter their outcome, you can never be separated from the love of God in Christ Jesus. Don't believe anyone who tells you otherwise. You don't have to clean yourself up, turn your life around, or be in a better mood. You don't have to do a thing. You are met by love, right here and right now. No matter how you feel, the love of Christ is yours. As David said in Psalm 139, "even there you would guide me. With your right hand you would hold me."

□ Act of Courage

Invite God into your messy life. Don't wait until you feel put together. Come as you are and be met by the river of his love.

Resurrection Life

Christ's resurrection is your resurrection too. This is why we are to yearn for all that is above, for that's where Christ sits enthroned at the place of all power, honor, and authority!

COLOSSIANS 3:1 TPT

Just as Christ was resurrected from the grave to life, so will we be. We will join him in his kingdom. What a beautiful hope! Let's live with our eyes focused on him, our values aligned with his, and our hearts open to his mercy and kindness. What we are filled with, we will overflow to the world around us. May we be filled with his love, peace, joy, hope, and truth.

When our longings are met in Christ, there is no end to the fulfillment we will find. Though our dreams may shift and change as we grow and mature in this life, God's incredible love never diminishes. It does not ebb; it is an overflowing waterfall at every turn and in every moment. As it rushes over us, we are revived in his life within us.

When the world seems too heavy, remember what awaits you in the fullness of Christ's kingdom.

Vision to Believe

We walk by faith, not by sight.

2 CORINTHIANS 5:7 CSB

When our expectations are not met in reality, it can be incredibly disheartening. When the wait seems to draw out, it can feel like we should give up. When our circumstances overwhelm our hope with the heaviness of challenges, who isn't even a little discouraged? Nothing is too difficult for God, and he is never taken by surprise.

Whether we recognize it or not, we try to figure out what God's promises will look like in our lives. Sometimes we don't have to stretch our imaginations far. But God's ways, his timing, and his purposes look differently than we can fathom with our limited understanding. Let's raise our faith to meet the incredible nature of our God, not diminish our understanding of God based on the challenges of our circumstances. When we make this adjustment, we are able to let go a little more, walking by faith and not by what we see.

☐ *Act of Courage*

Even when your days are hard, believe what God says. Trust his promises and wait on him. His love will fuel your faith. And remember, even a small kernel of faith can move a mountain.

Strong Love

Christ will make his home in your hearts as you trust in him. Your roots will grow down into God's love and keep you strong. And may you have the power to understand, as all God's people should, how wide, how long, how high, and how deep his love is. May you experience the love of Christ, though it is too great to understand fully.

EPHESIANS 3:17-19 NLT

How deeply do you understand the love of God? Do you see limits where God says there are none? Do you put barriers on his grace, where he has already broken them down? A great place to go back to over and over again is to the life, ministry, and teachings of Jesus. His love is a picture of the Father's love. Read his words, letting the wonders of his miracles and lessons broaden your expectations of his love in your own life.

There is always more to discover in Christ. Let your roots grow down into the life-giving soil of his mercy. Let his kindness draw you ever closer to him. Don't be afraid of what you will find there. He is better than you can imagine!

☐ Act of Courage

Dare to believe God's love is even better, brighter, and more forgiving than what you have yet experienced.

Lifegiving Wisdom

The excellence of knowledge is that wisdom gives life to those who have it.

ECCLESIASTES 7:12 NKJV

Wisdom is a protector. She offers a perspective we cannot attain on our own. The life-giving understanding she gives is more generous than the knowledge that is found in halls of higher learning. Wisdom is full of peace, joy, and love. It is grounded in truth. It is not anxious nor is it confusing.

May we look to the clarity of the Spirit's revelations as we make our decisions. May we trust the leading of the Lord in our hearts, minds, and lives as we submit to his kingdom wisdom as our guiding value in this life. There is so much life—abundant life!—in the wisdom of God. May we not be complacent in learning from the Lord and may pride not keep us stuck in limited ways of thinking. In God's wisdom, there is always opportunity to expand in our understanding.

❑ Act of Courage

Take time to dig into the knowledge that makes your heart and understanding come alive!

Good Friends

Do not be fooled:
"Bad friends will ruin good habits."

1 CORINTHIANS 15:33 NCV

Just as bad friends can ruin good habits, so can good friends encourage better ones. Good friends respect our boundaries and also encourage us to be the best version of ourselves. They won't let us settle for less than we are worth. They won't try to drag us into unhealthy situations. Good friends build us up, they don't tear us down.

Who in your life makes you feel seen, heard, and challenged to get closer to Christ? Who do you leave feeling better than before you were with them? These are good signs to pay attention to. This is not to say good friends won't push our buttons at times or challenge us in ways that can feel uncomfortable. Relationships are not perfect, but they should feel reciprocal, respectful, and enjoyable most of the time.

☐ *Act of Courage*

Spend more time with the people who encourage you to be your best self while still accepting you as you are. Spend less time with people who sabotage your efforts to grow.

Love In Action

If someone has enough money to live well and sees a brother or sister in need but shows no compassion— how can God's love be in that person?

1 JOHN 3:17 NLT

Love is not love that does not show itself in actions. Love follows through. Love makes others feel seen, heard, and important. When was the last time you heard a friend express a need and then surprised them by meeting it? Perhaps it was a bid for more time alone, and you offered to take their kids for an afternoon. Maybe they mentioned they were discouraged, and you sent them flowers. Love does not just hear; it listens and then acts.

It is important that we not only do this for the people in our direct circles, but also for those in our greater community. Compassion compels us to act. May we be so in tune with the love of God and so filled with his affection that it moves our hearts to help others. And may we not only wait for the feeling but put love into practice no matter our mood!

□ *Act of Courage*

When someone expresses a need you can meet, do it without hesitation today.

Tender Hearts

"Be careful that you never allow your hearts to grow cold. Remain passionate and free from anxiety and the worries of this life. Then you will not be caught off guard by what happens."

LUKE 21:34 TPT

What happens when a heart grows cold? Perhaps you think of people who seem disconnected or unfeeling toward those in need. Maybe you picture a rich person who refuses to give back to their communities but separates themselves in a kingdom of their own making. Love keeps our hearts soft. Thankfully we do not have to do this work on our own.

In Ezekiel 36:26, the Lord says, "I will give you a new heart, and I will put a new spirit in you. I will take out your stony, stubborn heart and give you a tender, responsive heart" (NLT). The Lord melts the frigidness of our unforgiving hearts and offers us hearts of flesh that respond to his merciful heart. We are connected to him, spirit to Spirit. May we not neglect this tremendous gift!

☐ Act of Courage

Give God your worries today and let God's compassion move you in whatever way you feel pulled to live out his love.

Active Trust

The king was overjoyed and gave orders to take Daniel out of the den. When Daniel was brought up from the den, he was found to be unharmed, for he trusted in his God.

DANIEL 6:23 CSB

What an interesting reaction the king had towards Daniel's death-defying experience. The king clearly had not wanted to throw Daniel into the lion's den, and yet he had to follow the official law of the land. He rejoiced the next morning when Daniel was discovered alive and unharmed after a night alone with hungry lions.

Daniel's accusers were proven to be in the wrong because of this mighty miracle. God sent an angel to shut the mouths of the lions, and the power of God was on display, not only for Daniel, but for the king as well. May we trust the Lord to guard us in the same way. When we are accused, may we put our hope in God's help. He knows the truth, and he will make sure others do too.

☐ Act of Courage

Trust God with the situations where you are unfairly accused of doing wrong. He will come through for you! Give him all your worries about it.

Tell the Truth

Do not lie to one another, since you laid aside the old self with its evil practices, and have put on the new self who is being renewed to a true knowledge.

COLOSSIANS 3:9-10 NASB

It is good to be honest with one another. May we have the courage to speak the truth, even when it feels uncomfortable. May we lay down the need to please everyone and instead live with integrity. May we choose the better, yet harder, path of honesty. Let's not tell lies to avoid conflict or to protect ourselves or others. The truth is worth telling, and any accusation because of it is unfounded.

There is a tremendous kindness that is offered in telling the truth; however, if we speak our opinion just to be heard, it is not the same thing. May we be people who value loving God, others, and ourselves well enough that we do not try to hide the truth but offer it as an act of courage.

❏ Act of Courage

When asked questions today, don't try to shape shift your answers depending upon whom you are talking to or how they might perceive you. Simply be honest.

What You Do

Be angry and do not sin;
do not let the sun go down on your anger.

EPHESIANS 4:26 ESV

Anger is an emotion everyone experiences. It is not a sin
to be angry. Do you know that? Even Jesus got angry! He
flipped tables over in the temple, and he shouted at those
who were misrepresenting the Father in a place dedicated
to worshiping him. Anger can be a really useful emotion
if we learn to look at it as a tool. What was at the root of
Jesus' anger? What is at the root of yours?

Anger can be clarifying, or it can be destructive. Let's get
curious about the things that set us off and attempt to
understand the underlying values that are being broken
which trigger anger in us. Why does that person who cut
in front of you while you were driving make you so mad?
Perhaps you have people in your life that take advantage
of you and refuse to see you. It is worth letting the Lord
show you what is going on in your heart when anger arises.
You are not a monster for being angry. There is probably a
boundary or value being crossed when you do! It is what
you do with your anger that matters.

❏ *Act of Courage*

*Find an outlet for your anger
where there is no shame involved.*

Courage to Grieve

"Now is your time of grief, but I will see you again and you will rejoice, and no one will take away your joy."

JOHN 16:22 NIV

There is a time for everything, Ecclesiastes says that there is a time to weep and a time to laugh, a time to mourn and a time to dance. Do you despise your grief, or do you embrace it? Whether or not you try to avoid it, you cannot escape it. Instead of trying to rush past the mourning, you must move through when you experience loss and accept that it is worth your surrender.

This is no small thing, and it is not easy. It takes courage to accept the cycles of grief as a natural part of life. There is no formula or blueprint to getting through your grief, but there is comfort available to you through that season. Be gentle with yourself, especially through the expectations you put upon yourself in times of mourning. Your capacity may be more limited, but your experience of love is not. Let the grief show what is true: what you lost matters.

☐ Act of Courage

Instead of trying to avoid the suffering that comes with being human, let yourself feel what is true. Jesus will meet you in it.

Strength to Wait

The LORD is good to those who wait for Him,
To the soul who seeks Him.

LAMENTATIONS 3:25 NKJV

When you set your heart to seek the Lord, it is good practice to grow in patience. There is so much give and take in every relationship, including the one we have with the Lord. Though he is always with us, it does not mean he works as our society does in a commodity economy. He is not the God of instant gratification. He is the God who fulfills us with the overwhelming goodness of his presence. Yet sometimes we have to wait on him.

When was the last time you took time to wait without an agenda on the timing of the Lord? Spending time in his presence, worshiping him, and inviting him to do what he wills is a beautiful practice to incorporate into the care of our souls. When the waiting seems to grow, so will the satisfaction when the answer comes.

☐ Act of Courage

Spend twenty minutes with the Lord turning your attention to his presence and inviting him to meet with you. Wait on him, and as you end your quiet time, let your heart remain open to him.

September

The LORD is my light and my salvation;
Whom shall I fear?
The LORD is the strength of my life;
Of whom shall I be afraid?

PSALM 27:1 NKJV

Witnesses of Power

"You will receive power when the Holy Spirit comes upon you. And you will be my witnesses, telling people about me everywhere—in Jerusalem, throughout Judea, in Samaria, and to the ends of the earth."

ACTS 1:8 NLT

It's no coincidence that Jesus declared that his people would receive power through the Holy Spirit *before* they would share about him with people everywhere. Though most of his disciples went on to be apostles, building the church throughout the ancient world, the news of Christ would have become storied lore as time went on. That is, without the power of the Holy Spirit there wouldn't have been apostles spreading the accurate Word of God. The Holy Spirit is given to each believer in the same measure. Through fellowship with the Spirit, we are able to experience and know the power of Christ's love in our lives. It is the power to transform our hearts, to live with integrity, and to walk in the ways—and miracles—of Christ.

We do not have to contrive a thing. We do not have to pretend. Let's wait on the Spirit to fill us and fuel our passion. Let's give him space to move in our hearts and minds.

☐ *Act of Courage*

Spend time in the presence of God asking him to fill you with his power and move in miraculous love.

Wisdom in Warning

Don't consider him as an enemy,
but warn him as a brother.

2 THESSALONIANS 3:15 CSB

Paul instructed the believers in Thessalonica to not treat their brothers and sisters in faith as enemies. Differences of opinion, action, and submission to the law of Christ's love do not give us the right to separate ourselves in our minds or hearts. When we see how others who claim to love God and follow him are not aligning with Jesus, may we choose to confront those issues in love.

When we seek to understand where others are coming from, when we approach conversations with humble hearts and a willingness to truly listen, others can tell. When we decide that offense is ours to use to coldly cut others off, we do not leave room for the generous grace of God to move. May we tell the truth always in love, and also lay down our assumptions of others in favor of asking them questions and providing our own perspectives after we have taken the time to truly listen. There is wisdom in warning others in love, and there is also wisdom in approaching them as family.

❏ *Act of Courage*

When you feel your defenses going up around certain Christians, instead of withdrawing, lean in with honesty and integrity.

Childlike

Jesus called for the children, saying, "Let the little children come to me. Don't stop them, because the kingdom of God belongs to people who are like these children."

LUKE 18:16 NCV

Have you ever been around a highly educated person who used their knowledge to make everyone around them feel inferior? This is not wisdom, nor is it the way of Christ. With innocence and curiosity, children move in the world with a sort of transparency which can be lost with age. Jesus never turned the children away. He welcomed their rambunctiousness and unfiltered questions.

Have you learned to hide your curiosity from your friends and family? Have you been conditioned to only ask certain types of questions or show specific emotions around others? There is grace in maturity, and there is wisdom in discernment, but we are never meant to lose our childlike wonder. May you rediscover the innocence of your childhood self, and may you welcome it as freely as Christ does!

☐ *Act of Courage*

Let your curiosity lead you today and ask Jesus all the questions. Don't temper yourself around him.
Be yourself, freely, as messy as it may feel.

Embodied Spirituality

While they were eating, He took some bread, and after a blessing He broke it, and gave it to them, and said, "Take it; this is My body."

MARK 14:22 NASB

Jesus wanted his disciples to practice spirituality, not only in the realm of mind, heart, soul, and spirit, but also in tangible, embodying practices. What we have come to call communion is a custom that involves our senses: our taste, smell, and touch. When we hold the bread before consuming it, we remember the body of Christ.

In modern western Christianity, many of us have lost the connection between our bodies and our faith. May we lean into the mystery of traditions that allow us to incorporate all of our senses in worship. When we eat our food, move our bodies, and interact with others, may we do it all with the awareness of Jesus as a human who came to earth. He ate, drank, walked, slept, played, rested, and ultimately died. Let's meditate on that, as we incorporate embodied practices into our devotional times.

☐ *Act of Courage*

Take communion even if you are by yourself. Use whatever you have on hand, not worrying about being overly correct. Just connected to the Lord.

Continue to Try

I do not mean that I am already as God wants me to be. I have not yet reached that goal, but I continue trying to reach it and to make it mine. Christ wants me to do that, which is the reason he made me his.

PHILIPPIANS 3:12 NCV

Life, through all its ebbs and flows, ups and downs, is a journey. As long as we are breathing, we can continue to grow, learn, and be refined in the love of Christ. Failure is inevitable, so instead of letting it define our worth let's remember God gives more grace to help us. As many closed doors as we encounter, there are also open ones ready to welcome us.

God knows us through and through. We would not expect a three-year-old to have the self-control of a thirty-year-old, so why don't we also give ourselves grace to keep trying and growing? God does not expect more of us than is possible to attain. He loves us, whether we get it right 10 percent or 90 percent of the time. His mercy is unwavering. From the solid foundation of his love, let's have the courage to try again as many times as it takes to break through our old habits.

❑ *Act of Courage*

Recognize where you still have the capacity to grow in love and integrity and ask the Lord for his help to do it.

Wisdom in Discretion

To quarrel with a neighbor is senseless.
Bite your tongue; be wise and keep quiet!

PROVERBS 11:12 TPT

The law of Christ's love is to offer mercy to others. There is never an excuse in God's kingdom to deride another person. How often do we feel justified in bashing another's character? Even if they deserve it due to their actions, our love does not grow when we participate in this kind of behavior.

May we have the courage to be as Jesus instructed us to be, loving others the way we love ourselves. We can disagree with others, but we don't need to fight about it or make them feel stupid. That is just arrogance in action. Jesus was as humble as they come; let's learn from his example. Let's keep quiet instead of lashing out, heeding the wisdom of Proverbs 17:28: "When even a fool bites his tongue he's considered wise. So shut your mouth when you are provoked—it will make you look smart."

☐ *Act of Courage*

When you are provoked in frustration, choose to keep your mouth shut and only talk about it when you have calmed down if you still feel the need.

Greater than Belief

The LORD of Armies says this: "Though it may seem impossible to the remnant of this people in those days, should it also seem impossible to me?"—this is the declaration of the LORD of Armies.

ZECHARIAH 8:6 CSB

Lack of faith is something talked about quite a bit in the Scriptures. Yet what is remarkable is God's overwhelming faithfulness even in the face of doubt among his people. What seems impossible to us with what little imagination we often have is not impossible to God. Nothing is impossible with him!

Do you have something the Lord keeps impressing upon your heart that feels impossible according to your current circumstances? God will be faithful to his Word and to his character regardless of your feelings about it. But wouldn't you much rather believe him and watch as he builds your faith for even greater things as he follows through?

☐ Act of Courage

Meditate on the miracles of God, Jesus, and the Holy Spirit in the Scriptures, and allow his power to increase your expectations of what he will do for you.

Mercy's Standard

> He saved us, not because of righteous things we had done, but because of his mercy. He saved us through the washing of rebirth and renewal by the Holy Spirit.
>
> TITUS 3:5 NIV

There is not a thing we can add to the powerful redemption of Christ's love. There is nothing we can do to take away from it either. He does not rely on our works, but rather on the overwhelming sufficiency of his mercy. Christ came to prove this point. It was never about what we offered God but what he offers us. Through our relationships with God, we experience the generosity of his grace at work within our lives.

What if we took the pressure to perform for God off of ourselves and simply received what he so freely offers us today? How would our thoughts change? Would we adjust our expectations for ourselves? Let's revel in the completely satisfying mercy of God that washes over us today, making us spotless before him. From this place, we can pursue what he puts within us to do without shame, obligation, or fear.

☐ *Act of Courage*

Instead of adding more things to do today to please God and others, receive the limitless love of God. Focus on receiving, and only receiving, in your time with him.

Behind Closed Doors

I'm trying my best to walk in the way of integrity
especially in my own home.
But I need your help!
I'm wondering, Lord, when will you appear?

PSALM 101:2 TPT

How we act behind closed doors is as important as how we act in public. Surely we all know this is true, but do we live that way? Integrity is not true unless it applies to every area of our lives. May we be authentic, honest, and honorable, choosing to follow Christ in our homes as persistently as we do in the communal places where we worship.

If this sounds like a tall order, we must remember it is by grace we have been saved, and it is through grace we continue to be refined. We need the help of God to be reliable. It can feel easier to offer mercy to those who don't continually test our patience. Integrity begins in the home. It is forged in the fires of our closest relationships. Let's be sure to prioritize how we love those closest to us before we venture to lay down our lives for strangers.

❏ *Act of Courage*

*Ask God for eyes to see where you can focus on
being consistent in your close relationships
and prioritize those things!*

Blessing Others

"The LORD bless you, and keep you;
The LORD make his face shine on you,
and be gracious to you;
The LORD lift up His countenance on you,
and give you peace."

NUMBERS 6:24-26 NASB

When we bless others, we benefit from it. When we choose to be agents of encouragement, our hearts grow in hope and satisfaction as we do. Our God is the God who turns curses into blessings (Nehemiah 13:2). May we partner with his heart in doing the same.

Jesus said, "Bless those who curse you, pray for those who are abusive to you…Give to everyone who asks of you, and whoever takes away what is yours, do not demand it back" (Luke 6:28, 30). Summing it up in verse thirty-six, Jesus instructed, "Be merciful, just as your Father is merciful." Choosing to bless others, not based on how they treat us but on how God treats us, is the way of Christ. Let's have the courage to follow his lead!

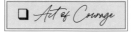

☐ Act of Courage

Choose to bless others today. If you don't know how to do it, use today's verse as your blessing. Blessing them in your heart counts as much as blessing them aloud.

Triumph in Hard Times

Even in the midst of all these things, we triumph over them all, for God has made us to be more than conquerors, and his demonstrated love is our glorious victory over everything!

ROMANS 8:37 TPT

Christ's victory isn't only apparent on our good days. The mercy of his victory over sin is most palpable when we are going through the wringer. This is good news for all of us. We cannot avoid pain in life, but we can still experience breakthrough! The Spirit of God is our comfort, our strength, and our help. The Spirit helps us in our weakness. Even when others try to tear us down, nothing can separate us from the love of God in Christ Jesus our Lord. That is our victory!

May you find no matter what you are facing or feeling today God's presence strengthens your heart. May you find that his peace overwhelms your fears. May you know the deeply abiding joy of his mercy and kindness for you. Oh, how he loves you!

☐ *Act of Courage*

Remember that nothing can separate you from the love of God today. No, nothing!

Clothed in Compassion

"Do not enter the city gate of my people in their time of trouble or laugh at their problems in their time of trouble. Do not take their treasures in their time of trouble."

OBADIAH 1:13 NCV

Have you ever found joy in another person's misery? Nothing could be further from the compassion of Christ. And yet we are human; each one of us. Once we understand how swiftly things can change in this life, we may find our hearts are more sober and quick to sympathize and console rather than be indifferent or rush to judgment.

There is a deep solidarity that happens naturally after we have experienced devastation in our own lives. When loss touches us, we are never the same. Even as our grief breaks our hearts open, God's love rushes in to fill that space. The more someone suffers, the more capacity for compassion they have. And yet each of us has room for it, here and now. We can choose to partner with God's love, or we can choose to separate ourselves in pride or self-protection. Let's always be on the side of mercy, for there we will find Christ every time.

☐ *Act of Courage*

Be respectful of others' pain,
and don't try to rush them through it.

Set Out Again

"Arise, my love, my beautiful one, and come away,
for behold, the winter is past;
the rain is over and gone.
The flowers appear on the earth,
the time of singing has come."

SONG OF SOLOMON 2:10-12 ESV

Long winters can cause us to feel isolated. It can seem as if the whole world has gone to sleep. The branches on the trees are bare, and the fields are covered with snow or brown grass. Plants go dormant, and many animals retreat. Even so, the barrenness of winter serves a purpose. With the turning of the seasons, we are reminded of the cycles of this life. Though winter cannot be avoided, neither can spring!

New life is always coming. It is around the corner. May you find your soul rises in hope as you sense the signs of your spiritual springtime. God is not finished with you. What felt like your end was just a new beginning. There is more to come, more life to live, and more joy to experience. Revel in the changes you find blossoming all around you. This is your time to bloom!

☐  Act of Courage

Look for where signs of new life are poking through in the mundane details of your life. Look ahead with hope!

Before You Ask

"Do not be like them. For your Father knows the things you have need of before you ask Him."

MATTHEW 6:8 NKJV

Who is it Jesus is instructing his followers to not be like? In the previous verse, Jesus says there is no need to repeat empty phrases like those who don't know God do. God doesn't tune in to listen when we say the right words. He is not far off or aloof. He already knows exactly what we need before we ask him.

This passage of Scripture is when Jesus teaches his disciples how to pray. This is where we find the Lord's Prayer. This is a good place to start if we don't know how else to do it. As with all things in Christ, it is through relationship that we find our souls satisfied. May we draw near to God, for he will draw near to us when we do. In fact, he is already closer than we think. When we pray, let's speak to him like a close friend; one who is sitting by us, ready to hear our hearts.

☐ *Act of Courage*

Pray with confidence today knowing you are heard.
Use the Lord's Prayer as a starting place
and open your heart to God.

Gifted by God

He has filled them with skill to do all the work of a gem
cutter; a designer; an embroiderer in blue, purple, and
scarlet yarn and fine linen; and a weaver. They can do
every kind of craft and design artistic designs.

EXODUS 35:35 CSB

Have you ever considered the talents you have are a gift
from God? What he has put in you is not meant to be
neglected but to be refined. We do not all have the same
gifts, and that is a good thing! In the diversity of our
talents, we can depend on and inspire each other. Artistic
gifts are as important as practical ones.

Have you neglected a passion that came easily to you in
your youth? Instead of trying to find more spiritual pursuits,
let the training and refining of these very things be your
spiritual offering! The one who filled you with skill is the one
who delights in your joyful exploration of your ability.

☐ Act of Courage

Make time to pursue the things that make you come alive.
What interests click for you? What comes easily?
Don't neglect these things, for God put them in you.

No More Division

He himself is our peace, who has made the two
groups one and has destroyed the barrier,
the dividing wall of hostility.

EPHESIANS 2:14 NIV

In Christ, Paul says in Ephesians, there is no more Jew or
Greek. There is no difference between any of the children
of God. There is not one chosen race or ethnicity who
receives the love of God. In Christ it is offered to all in the
same measure. All those who come to Christ are brothers
and sisters. There is no hierarchy in his kingdom.

Do we truly believe we are all equal? Do we live without
letting our biases keep us from seeing others in their full
humanity? There are no barriers between us in Christ;
only the ones we keep putting up ourselves. And this
is not the way of Christ. In him there is no difference in
class, gender, or race. Not to say that these differences
aren't represented in his kingdom; it just doesn't make any
difference in our liberation or in his love!

☐ Act of Courage

*When you recognize that you feel either better or worse
than someone else, remember Christ loves us all in the
same way! Choose to love without barriers just as he does.*

Perfect Unity

God has chosen you and made you his holy people. He loves you. So you should always clothe yourselves with mercy, kindness, humility, gentleness, and patience. Even more than all this, clothe yourself in love. Love is what holds you all together in perfect unity.

COLOSSIANS 3:12, 14 NCV

Love holds all the other virtues of Christ's kingdom together. It is what holds us as God's people, together. Where there is love, there is freedom. We know that God is love, so wherever he is, there is also all he offers through his Spirit. There is peace, joy, and hope. There is strength, comfort, and patience.

May we never grow tired of growing in active love toward God, toward others, and toward ourselves. When we clothe ourselves with mercy, kindness, humility, gentleness, and patience, we make ourselves approachable. We keep ourselves open to connection. This is important enough for us to fight against the urge to self-protect, hide, or judge.

❑ *Act of Courage*

Choose to lay down your judgments in favor of kindness, humility, and patience. Take unity seriously, and fight for love to always be at the forefront of your efforts.

Freed From the Past

To enjoy your work and accept your lot in life—
this is indeed a gift from God. God keeps such people
so busy enjoying life that they take no time to brood
over the past.

ECCLESIASTES 5:19-20 NLT

Life satisfaction goes hand in hand with accepting what
your life looks like. What are the enjoyable things you have
available to you right here and right now? It is easy to get
too far ahead of ourselves when considering what the
future holds. It's also just as easy to long for what was in
our past. We cannot go back, and we cannot control the
future, but we can appreciate what we have now.

It is a beautiful thing to cultivate enjoyment in the little
things. Perhaps we have become so caught up in looking
back or ahead we take for granted the gifts we have now.
What is a reality in your life you once longed and prayed
for? As you remember these things, may gratitude fill your
heart and refocus your attention on the gifts within your
present reality.

❑ Act of Courage

Make a list of what you have now that you once longed for.
As you go over it, thank God for each one. Go into
the rest of your day with gratitude for what is,
and release what is no longer.

Under No Circumstances

"How could a loving mother forget her nursing child and not deeply love the one she bore? Even if a there is a mother who forgets her child, I could never, no never, forget you."

ISAIAH 49:15 TPT

Often when we think of God, we think of him as Father. God is as much a mother to us as he is a father. Think of the most nurturing woman you know . What kind of love does she display to those in her life? She is a picture of the nurturing and forgiving love of God. There is nothing we could ever do to lose that love.

Just as a good mother is connected to her child through the unconditional love that was birthed in the womb, God is even more connected to us through the love in which he knit us together. Even if our own mothers were to forsake us and turn their backs on us, God never would. First John 4:16 illuminates the blessing of this kind of unfettered connection: "We have come into an intimate experience with God's love, and we trust in the love he has for us."

☐ *Act of Courage*

Come to Love, knowing that you are always accepted as you are. Receive directly from the Source of your life, and may you know the all-consuming courage of being seen, known, and loved.

Powerful Weakness

"My grace is sufficient for you, for my power is made perfect in weakness." Therefore I will boast all the more gladly of my weaknesses, so that the power of Christ may rest upon me. For the sake of Christ, then, I am content with weaknesses, insults, hardships, persecutions, and calamities. For when I am weak, then I am strong.

2 CORINTHIANS 12:9-10 ESV

How often do you perceive your weaknesses as something worth boasting about? Do you fight the feeling of shame over your natural limitations? In a society that praises busyness and hustle it can be a downright fight to embrace the weakness of our humanity. When our limitations end, God's never do. May we surrender our weaknesses, allowing the grace of God to empower us.

Sometimes, the best thing we can do is to take a break. Rest is *restorative*. It is necessary for us. When we have no more to give, God does not tell us we are being silly, or we should keep going regardless. What an insensitive Father he would be if he did. No, he restores us in his perfect peace and carries us when our legs give way beneath us.

☐ *Act of Courage*

Instead of pushing yourself when you are tired, take a break and invite the Spirit of peace to minister to you.

Beauty of Faith

Though you have not seen him, you love him; though not seeing him now, you believe in him, and you rejoice with inexpressible and glorious joy.

1 PETER 1:8 CSB

Faith could be described as a strong belief in God that is based on spiritual apprehension rather than proof. There is something mystical about this. Though we do not see God, we love him. We experience his love though we cannot hold it in our hands. Let's lean into the beauty of the mystery and fellowship spirit to Spirit and heart to heart with our Maker.

Faith requires trust. God is faithful, true, and trustworthy. He is love itself, the source of all life, and he redeems what no one else can. Let's continue to throw our anchor of hope in the ocean of his mercy. He is kind and good; he is just and powerful. As we believe his promises that align with his nature, our hearts are bolstered in peace that passes understanding.

 Act of Courage

Instead of trying to figure God out today, choose to trust him. Invite the Holy Spirit to fill you with peace, joy, and hope as you choose to rest in his faithfulness.

Uncontainable

"Will God indeed dwell on the earth? Behold, heaven and the highest heaven cannot contain You, how much less this house which I have built!"

1 KINGS 8:27 NASB

When Solomon oversaw the building of the temple, he recognized that such a small dwelling could not contain God. The Creator, who is everywhere and yet cannot be held, could not be confined to one place. Yet the same God who came to the Israelites through a pillar of fire by night and a cloud during the day in order to guide them through the wilderness, would dwell in the holy of holies.

God is omnipresent. This means he can be everywhere at the same time. His unbounded presence meets us each wherever we are. Jesus removed the need to find God in sacred spaces. The veil that separated the holy of holies from the rest of the temple was torn on the day he died. He provided access for each of us, and that invitation still stands today. May we encounter the uncontainable God as we go about our ordinary lives, for his Spirit is with us wherever we go!

☐ *Act of Courage*

Invite God to meet you in the most ordinary aspects of your day.

Courage to Act

"Be strong and courageous, and do the work. Don't be afraid or discouraged, for the Lord God, my God, is with you. He will not fail you or forsake you. He will see to it that all the work related to the Temple of the Lord is finished."

1 CHRONICLES 28:20 NLT

Courage is required for action. What courage do we need to stay in our comfortable lifestyles or homes, hiding from the world? No, strength and courage are needed as we do the work God has given us to do. It takes courage to love those who make it really hard to like them. It takes strength to persevere when we would rather give up.

May we have fresh vision and courage to do the work that is uniquely ours to do. If we wait for others to join us, we may be waiting forever. Let's take the steps that are ours to take, and let's consistently work toward the goals we have before us. In all things we get to partner with the Spirit of God and incorporate his kingdom values into our work. So, let's do it!

☐ *Act of Courage*

Take the next step you've been hesitant to take, trusting that God will meet you in it and show you where to go after that.

Ever Increasing

We ought always to thank God for you, brothers and sisters, and rightly so, because your faith is growing more and more, and the love all of you have for one another is increasing.

2 THESSALONIANS 1:3 NIV

Paul began this letter by expressing his gratitude that the Thessalonians' faith and love were actively growing. At the end his first letter, he closed by praying for them, "May the Lord make your love increase and overflow for each other and everyone else, just as ours does for you" (3:12). This goes to show there is always more to grow in!

If we give ourselves to anything, may it be to increase our faith in God and our love for others. The love of God is always expanding, and we can always be growing in it as well. May we never grow apathetic in comfort, for relationships require engagement and intentionality. May we continually embrace the opportunity to love others in ever-expansive ways just as Christ loves us.

 ☐ Act of Courage

Instead of making excuses for why you don't have to engage with others, look for tangible and practical ways to love others today.

Courage to Follow

> "You shall walk after the LORD your God and fear Him, and keep His commandments and obey His voice; you shall serve Him and hold fast to Him."

DEUTERONOMY 13:4 NKJV

What vision keeps you moving forward in life? Above all else, where is your focus when you look to the future? May your attention be on the Lord your God, who faithfully leads you wherever you go. His ways are better than your own. His wisdom considers what your limited logic misses. Keep his ways, obey his voice, and hold onto him.

It takes courage to follow God, and yet he knows the best ways to guide you. He can see into your future, whereas you cannot see beyond this moment. Nothing is a surprise to him, and he cannot be fooled, tricked, or controlled. Look to him, and you can have confidence that no matter what kind of circumstances you walk through, he is leading you in love, in redemption, and in the security of his presence.

☐ *Act of Courage*

Before you make any decisions to act today, ask the Lord what he would have you do. If you sense him leading you, follow.

Great Confidence

We can say with great confidence: "I know the Lord is for me and I will never be afraid of what people may do to me!"

HEBREWS 13:6 TPT

Even when faced with death, the apostles, prophets, and followers of Yahweh did not back down. God promised as verse five of this chapter in Hebrews says, "I will never leave you alone, never! And I will not loosen my grip on your life!" Though we cannot control what that looks like in our lives, we can trust God is with us through it all. His Spirit is incessant.

May the root of our confidence be in God's care of us. Even if our bodies deteriorate and others curse us, God will not abandon us. His presence is full of peace, love, and joy. May we know what it is to experience the comfort of his nearness even in our suffering. May we join with those who have gone before us, including the psalmist who said, "In all of my affliction I find great comfort in your promises, for they have kept me alive" (Psalm 119:50).

☐ *Act of Courage*

Look to the Lord when you are afraid, inconvenienced, or overwhelmed today.

No Unnecessary Oaths

My brothers and sisters, above all, do not use an oath when you make a promise. When you mean yes, say only yes, and when you mean no, say only no so you will not be judged guilty.

James 5:12 NCV

In our modern culture, we have lost the understanding of the power of an oath. In Biblical times, a vow could not be broken without severe consequences. God's promise is based on his character, and he cannot go against it. Let's not make promises we have no intention of keeping, and let's not throw around an oath without taking it seriously.

It is much better for us to simply say yes or no. Let's not swear to something we cannot uphold. We become hypocrites when we do this. Jesus instructed in Matthew 5:34, 36 that we, "Never swear an oath. Don't even swear by your own head, because you cannot make one hair on your head become white or black." We are to say yes when we mean yes and no when we mean no. It is actually simple, so let's not complicate things by trying to please others and instead get ourselves into trouble!

 ☐ Act of Courage

Do not agree to anything you have no intention of following through on. It takes courage to uphold your own integrity.

Come to Jesus

Jesus told him, "I am the way, the truth, and the life.
No one comes to the Father except through me."

JOHN 14:6 CSB

Whatever you are searching for can be found in Jesus. Are you looking for belonging? He welcomes you with open arms. Are you looking for wisdom to help you live your best life? He has solutions that pertain to your problems. Are you looking for where to invest your resources? His generosity will instruct your own.

Whatever you are carrying, bring it to Jesus. If you have heavy burdens of worry, he will gladly take them as you offer them to him. If you have passion for helping others, he will help you to direct it with compassion. Jesus remains the way, the truth, and the life. He leads the way to the Father, where you will find belonging as his child. Don't hesitate today. Come to Jesus and bring him all that you are. He loves to receive you.

☐ *Act of Courage*

Be honest with what is weighing you down and bring it to Jesus today. Let him minister to the places you try to keep hidden from others. You cannot scare him away!

Courage to Hear

> "The hearts of this people have grown dull. Their ears are hard of hearing, And their eyes they have closed, Lest they should see with their eyes and hear with their ears, Lest they should understand with their hearts and turn, So that I should heal them."
>
> MATTHEW 13:15 NKJV

Jesus said in verse twelve of this same chapter that everyone who listens with an open heart is able to receive progressively more revelation until they have more than enough. Open and teachable hearts are what keep our ears attuned to the Spirit. If we think we already know all we need to know, we shut ourselves off from hearing what would challenge our perceptions. How can we hear the word of the Lord if we are not willing to change our minds?

It takes courage to humbly remain open to changing our opinions on things that are not set in stone. If we will be teachable and willing to learn from others, then we make room for our own transformation and for the love of God to lead us beyond the borders of our limited experiences. May we have the courage to keep our hearts open!

 ❏ Act of Courage

Ask God to reveal an area of thinking that does not align with his kingdom values and be willing to change it when you see the light of his truth.

Builders of Hope

Each of us should please our neighbors for their good,
to build them up.

ROMANS 15:2 NIV

When was the last time you did something for someone else, purely to bless them and without an agenda, an expectation of return, or a point to prove? Today's verse is so simple, and yet it is not lived out by many. May we reach outside of the self-serve society that we are entrenched in and learn to give to others in order to build them up.

The economy of the kingdom is generous, meeting others' needs with the understanding that this is how we care for one another. God is capable of providing for all of our needs, and often he does. But much of the time this is done through others. May we take the generosity of God seriously, giving freely and receiving when we are also in need. It is a cycle of provision that builds everyone up!

☐ Act of Courage

Rather than relying on the ideology of self-sufficiency, which is not promoted by Scripture, look for ways to meet the practical needs of others, and then do it as an act of God's generous love in action.

October

"I leave the gift of peace with you—
my peace. Not the kind of fragile peace
given by the world, but my perfect peace.
Don't yield to fear or be troubled in your
hearts—instead, be courageous!"

JOHN 14:27 TPT

Our Great Keeper

The LORD will be your confidence
and will keep your foot from being caught.

PROVERBS 3:26 NASB

Proverbs 3:25 prefaces today's verse by saying, "Do not be afraid of sudden danger, nor of trouble from the wicked when it comes." When trouble comes, the Lord will be our confidence and will keep us from being ensnared by others' traps. He is reliable in powerful mercy, and he will always come through in strength.

When you feel the weight of worry settling on your mind, look to the Lord. When you feel the burden of anxiety rising within your chest, turn your attention to your very near help. The Spirit lifts the crushing heaviness of discomfort and settles your heart with peace. May you know the great relief it is to be confident in your King and Savior. He is with you!

☐ *Act of Courage*

Give your worries to Jesus today and ask him to give you the all-surpassing peace of his presence in order to build your confidence in him. What he offers is light and life-giving.

Sweet Rest

In peace I will both lie down and sleep;
for you alone, O LORD, make me dwell in safety.

PSALM 4:8 ESV

Even in the midst of the chaos in this world, we can rest peacefully in the presence of God. It does not mean we are disconnected from compassion when we sleep soundly at night. May we learn to lay down what we cannot change as we go to bed at night, trusting God to do what he will. We can trust him to be there for those concerns we cannot solve.

In an age of information overload, there is so much by which we feel burdened. Wars in distant places, natural disasters which seem to be increasing in frequency, always concerning news about people. This, compounded by the troubles that are closer to home only serve to heighten the feeling that we should be doing more. But at the end of the day, there's only so much we can do, and so much we can't. Let's make a practice of letting go of what we cannot control and trusting God to guide us in the ways we can help. But as we release it, let's give ourselves the permission to rest; really rest.

☐ Act of Courage

*If you struggle to sleep, write down everything
that comes to mind, and release what you can to God.
Delegate the rest for tomorrow.*

Courage to Worship

"You are worthy, our Lord and God, to receive glory, honor, and power, for you created all things, and by your plan they were created and exist."

REVELATION 4:11 TPT

When we come face-to-face with the glory of the Lord, we will bow down in worship just as the angels and elders are described as doing in the book of Revelation. We won't do this because we're obligated to, but because we are compelled to! No one has seen the fullness of God's glory and lived. And yet, many have seen glimpses.

May we find the courage to worship the Lord in Spirit and in truth while we are living by faith. Let's give him honor, not only through our songs, prayers, and acts of worship, but through our surrendered lives. He who created all things created each of us in his image. We are unique reflections of the indescribable beauty of his being! No matter what we feel about ourselves in our lowest moments, we are carriers of his glory.

 ☐ Act of Courage

Set aside time to worship God in whatever way feels like a true expression of you today and give him your full attention during that time.

God Will Do It

"I will deal severely with all who have oppressed you. I will save the weak and helpless ones; I will bring together those who were chased away. I will give glory and fame to my former exiles, wherever they have been mocked and shamed."

ZEPHANIAH 3:19 NLT

Oppression in all of its forms is unacceptable to God. He will not hear the excuses of powerful people looking to escape the consequences of their actions. He deals in mercy, and he also deals in justice. He can love us thoroughly and still correct us.

When we feel overlooked or abandoned by those who are supposed to support and protect us, may we remember that God is our defender. He will not let the weak and helpless ones waste away. Let's be careful about who we align ourselves with. God says we should look out for the vulnerable ones in society, so let's not turn blind eyes to them and support those who oppress them.

☐ Act of Courage

Ask God if there is any area where you are out of alignment with his purposes and heart when it comes to the weak and helpless ones.

Guard against Jealousy

> Don't let your heart envy sinners;
> instead, always fear the LORD.
> For then you will have a future,
> and your hope will not be dashed.
>
> PROVERBS 23:17-18 CSB

Jealousy is not a fruit of the Spirit. In fact, it can distract us from what truly matters and make our hearts bitter toward one another. We may find ourselves dissatisfied if we compare our lives with others. It's important to remember that no one's life is perfect. You may be living someone else's dream all the while feeling like you just want what your friend has.

What is a helpful way to guard against envy? One of the simplest ways is to cultivate a heart of gratitude. Another is to form a connection with others based on compassion. When we hear what others are going through, we get a better picture of the fact that everyone struggles. Even those who appear to have it all together have trials. Let's give up the quest for perfection and embrace the beauty of the messy parts of life. Let's connect with one another in authentic ways where we can show up as ourselves.

☐ Act of Courage

Every time you begin to compare your life with others in a negative way, list three things you love about your life.

Always Satisfied

Be full of joy in the Lord always.
I have learned to be satisfied with the things I have
and with everything that happens.

PHILIPPIANS 4:4, 11 NCV

How was Paul able to truthfully say that he was satisfied
no matter what his circumstances were? He said that he
learned to be at peace whether in plenty or in deficit, in
feast or in famine. How? It was because his satisfaction was
much deeper than his circumstances which could change
with the shifting winds. It was a soul satisfaction that the
Spirit offered.

Through fellowship with the Holy Spirit, we have the same
presence of peace, joy, patience, kindness, and hope at
work within us. He can teach us how to be satisfied with
what we have so our gratitude grows with each day. He
can offer us the fullness of joy found in knowing God is
with us. What a beautiful thing to attain to!

☐ Act of Courage

*Keep a gratitude journal for the next month and write
down everything you are thankful for each day.
Rate your level of satisfaction with life each week and
evaluate if it helped you at the end of the month.*

Harmonious Humility

Live in harmony with one another. Do not be proud,
but be willing to associate with people of low position.
Do not be conceited.

ROMANS 12:16-18 NIV

How important is it to you that you live in harmony
with others? Though you will not always get along with
everyone, it is important to still act in love. This does not
mean withholding the truth when repairs need to be made
or confrontation needs to happen, but it does mean you do
it with an open heart.

God does not judge people based on their appearance. Do
you? To truly follow Christ, you must be willing to associate
with people from all positions and levels of society. Do
not show favor to people based on how they are dressed
or how you assume they identify. Love is love is love.
Take your cues from Christ, who ate with sinners and tax
collectors. He was not afraid to be seen with them, so
neither should you worry what others will think of you.

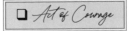

☐ *Act of Courage*

*Have a conversation with someone you
might normally avoid today.*

Taking Up Your Cross

"Whoever wants to be my disciple must deny themselves and take up their cross daily and follow me."

LUKE 9:23 NIV

What does it look like to take up your cross and follow Jesus? Does it not include surrendering to the ways of Christ and following his example? If we truly do this, then we have to know how Jesus lived, and how he instructed us to live, and how to follow his commands. How well do we know the gospels? Do we really understand what living for Christ means?

When we lay down our own preferences, clothe ourselves in compassion, and incorporate the values of God's kingdom as our own, we follow him well. It is not a life of luxury or ease he calls us to. It is not one of comfort or exclusivity either. The love of God opens us up to interacting with those we would never have chosen on our own. And yet, we are the better for it every time. May we embrace the cross of Christ and follow him wherever he leads us.

☐ *Act of Courage*

Read through the Sermon on the Mount (Matthew 5-7) and write down what stands out to you as applicable to surrendering your life to the Lord.

Not an Orphan

"I will not leave you as orphans;
I am coming to you."

JOHN 14:18 NASB

Jesus promised not to leave his disciples as orphans. Little could they anticipate he was actually saying that he would die and then rise again three days later. He came to them after he was resurrected and promised that the Holy Spirit would come to them and never leave them.

Jesus will come again. He promised he would. While we wait for his return may we find strength in the community of his kingdom on this earth. Hebrews 10:24-25 says, "Let's consider how to encourage one another in love and good deeds, not abandoning our own meeting together... but encouraging one another, and all the more as you see the day drawing near." There is wisdom in gathering with brothers and sisters in Christ and supporting one another in love and encouragement.

Spend time with believers this week.
It can help remind you that you are not alone!

Persistent Patience

The Lord is not slow in doing what he promised—the way some people understand slowness. But God is being patient with you. He does not want anyone to be lost, but he wants all people to change their hearts and lives.

2 PETER 3:9 NCV

It is because of God's goodness that he is patient with us. What we would rush into, God gives us space to strengthen our character. God is not slow in doing what he promised. This is as true today as it was when Peter first wrote the above verse. God is not behind, and neither are we.

May we see patience for what it is—a gift from a good, good God. He doesn't want anyone to miss their chance at coming alive in his love. He doesn't want us to flounder under the weight of anything we are not equipped to handle. He sees beyond the demands of our childlike tendency toward instant gratification. He takes into consideration what we miss in our short-sightedness. And thank God for that! May we learn to lean into the waiting with patience, gratitude, and peace.

❏ *Act of Courage*

Thank God for the things you are still waiting on and ask for eyes to see the joys that are already a part of your life.

Pure Religion

*Pure and undefiled religion before God and the Father
is this: to visit orphans and widows in their trouble, and
to keep oneself unspotted from the world.*

JAMES 1:27 NKJV

The kind of devotion God wants from us is not hours spent isolated or fasting to beat our bodies into submission. He wants us to live lives of loving connection and care for others. Let's be those people who visit the vulnerable in their trouble. Let's persistently help meet the needs of others. Compassion grows when we connect with others and see the reality of their circumstances.

True spirituality makes a difference in the lives of orphans and widows. Let's not let the world's values corrupt us and keep us from reaching out to help those in need. Where we are taught to remain separated from those who are different than us, God calls us to break down barriers and treat everyone with kindness and mercy. His ways are always better than our own, so let's clothe ourselves in his compassion as we make intentional moves to connect with people.

☐ *Act of Courage*

*Take some time to consider which of the world's values
you need to abandon in favor of the values of Christ.*

Higher Trust

"Look at the proud! They trust in themselves, and their lives are crooked. But the righteous will live by their faithfulness to God."

HABAKKUK 2:4 NLT

Do we trust more in our own competence than we do God's faithfulness? In a world that values what is measurable by human standards, we leave little room for the ambiguous but important connections in nature, people, and God. May we remain humble in heart, ready to admit where our knowledge falls short.

Trusting God does not mean we abandon personal responsibility. It does not look like rejecting the hard realities of our lives. It means we hold the tension between what is experienced and what we cannot perceive. May we not elevate our own abilities by trusting in ourselves more than we do the powerful love of God that covers our weaknesses and transforms us from the inside out. Let's surrender and follow the Lord, for he is loyal and trustworthy!

☐ *Act of Courage*

When you don't understand something today, when you find it's above your ability to ascertain, ask the Lord to reveal his perspective and wisdom to you.

Triumphant Love

Now I live with the confidence that there is nothing in the universe with the power to separate us from God's love. I'm convinced that his love will triumph over death, life's troubles, fallen angels, or dark rulers in the heavens. There is nothing in our present or future circumstances that can weaken his love.

ROMANS 8:38 TPT

When we are convinced of God's love for us—the kind of love that covers sins—it liberates us from shame and fear and offers generous grace for our mistakes. We stand on the grounded confidence of Christ. It is from this place that we can build our lives on the solid foundation of who God is. His love will not be removed, and neither will we be moved from it.

More than anything else, let's give ourselves to knowing, receiving, and growing in the overwhelmingly good love of God. It is who God is, after all! We cannot go wrong when we live with love as our true north. Love is the foundation, it is the house we build, and the soil our roots grow deeply into. Christ's love is triumphant, and it is all-encompassing. Living with his love as the banner over our lives is a worthy pursuit!

☐ *Act of Courage*

Meditate on what the power of God's love looks like in your life.

Promised Rest

> The LORD replied, "My Presence will go with you, and I
> will give you rest."
>
> EXODUS 33:14 NIV

God not only promises to go with us, but he also promises to give us rest along the way. When we are overwhelmed with the journey that lies ahead of us, let's take God's Word to heart. His presence will be guiding us and providing respites in his love. Nothing is too much for God.

Do we push ourselves beyond the point of exhaustion thinking that's how things should be done? Not according to Scripture. God does not call us to burnout or to endless work. He set the precedent for time off in the beginning when he created the Sabbath. After creating the earth and everything in it, he spent a day admiring all he had made. May we, too, embrace the rhythms of rest that are so necessary to our health and growth.

When you are tired, take time off to rest. Even if it seems counterintuitive, rest will rejuvenate you for what is ahead.

Don't Go Backwards

We have freedom now, because Christ made us free.
So stand strong. Do not change and go back into the
slavery of the law.

GALATIANS 5:1 NCV

When was the last time you felt the freedom of Christ to live as your most authentic self? There are responsibilities in life we cannot avoid, but the obligations of love are life-giving. His love sets us free to walk in the light of his goodness and to choose how we will express our love to him.

Anyone who is familiar with the shadow of shame knows the feeling of being restricted. Christ did not set us free except for certain areas of our lives. His power sets us free from sin, shame, and fear. There is only light in his presence. He shines on the darkness and reveals what is hidden. His presence empowers us to stand strong in his love so we will not go back into the slavery of the law. Where shame beckons us to hide and shrink, let's move toward love that calls us to stand tall and grow toward the light!

☐ *Act of Courage*

Where you have felt yourself shrinking because of what others may think of you, allow yourself to blossom in safe spaces until you can do it everywhere and with everyone.

He Knows

God's firm foundation stands, bearing this seal: "The Lord knows those who are his," and, "Let everyone who names the name of the Lord depart from iniquity."

2 TIMOTHY 2:19 ESV

We don't have to worry about whether God sees our motivations. He knows those who are his. He knows what our hearts are drawn to. When we submit to the ways of Christ, we do not work for selfish gain but for the good of all. Let this be a challenge to us, and also let it be a reason to draw near to the Lord every moment.

Jesus said in John 10:14-15, "I am the good shepherd. I know my own and my own know me, just as the Father knows me and I know the Father; and I lay down my life for the sheep." It is not a mystery to the Lord who are his and who reject him. Instead of worrying about others and whether or not they submit to the Lord, let's take care of our own hearts, lives, and relationships. Let's focus on the only thing we can actually change by God's grace—ourselves.

☐ Act of Courage

Look at your own life—the splinter and plank analogy comes to mind from Matthew 7:5—and adjust your heart and actions before the Lord.

Age Doesn't Matter

Then I said, "Oh, Lord GOD! Behold, I do not know how to speak, Because I am a youth."
But the LORD said to me, "Do not say, 'I am a youth,' Because everywhere I send you, you shall go, And all that I command you, you shall speak. Do not be afraid of them, For I am with you to save you," declares the LORD.

JEREMIAH 1:6-8 NASB

God does not qualify people based on their age or their experience. He uses those who are willing. When God calls you to something, there is no use arguing with him that you lack the credentials. In the end, he will confirm that he is with you wherever you go. He will give you the words to speak. He will be your strength, even when others try to intimidate you.

Have you ever disqualified yourself from doing something that felt scary because you compared yourself with others who seem more capable? Trust the Lord when he leads you and remember he goes with you wherever you go. You are never alone!

☐ Act of Courage

Believe that what God has called you to, he will equip you for. Lean on his understanding more than on your own.

Generosity's Gift

If you offer yourself to the hungry,
and satisfy the afflicted one,
then your light will shine in the darkness,
and your night will be like noonday.

ISAIAH 58:10 CSB

Being generous does not only benefit those with whom we share our resources, but it also is a gift to us. There is something cathartic about helping someone just because we can. Even though we can't control our circumstances, we can choose what we do with what we have. When we practice generosity, we become like our Father who is limitless in practical acts of love!

When was the last time you offered to share your food with someone who is hungry? How about meeting the needs of someone down on their luck? We don't have to solve everyone's problems in order to make a difference. Small acts of kindness done with love can do wonders for a person's faith and hope.

☐ Act of Courage

Help meet a need today no matter how small and thank God for the opportunity to do it.

Endless Mercy

To the LORD our God belong mercy and forgiveness,
though we have rebelled against Him.

DANIEL 9:9 NKJV

Even when we rebel against God, we cannot change his nurturing nature. His love for us never changes. Consider the parable of the prodigal son (Luke 15:11-32). The son left his father's house to chase his whims. In fact, he squandered his inheritance away. Being destitute, he did what he could think of—return to his father's house and beg for a place as a servant.

What did the father do? Did he give him a stern lecture about how he should have known better? Did he think it over and require his son pay penance? Not even close! He ran out to meet him—which says that he was looking for him—wrapped him in his embrace and gave him his own robe. He threw a party in honor of his son's homecoming. This father was full of mercy and forgiveness, and so is ours. It is a clear picture of the goodness of his heart toward us.

☐ *Act of Courage*

Show mercy and forgiveness rather than give a lecture today. You may just show the Father's love by doing so.

Daily Encouragement

Encourage one another daily, as long as it is called "Today," so that none of you may be hardened by sin's deceitfulness.

HEBREWS 3:13 NIV

Even when we are going through times when things are hard, we can still encourage one another in God's love. As long as it is today, there is an opportunity to uplift each other. There is time to speak the truth. This moment, this lived experience, is truly all we have to work with. Let's use it wisely!

Who in your life is really good at encouragement? Make a point to reach out to them. Who do you know that needs some encouragement? Spend some time connecting with them even if it is a short time just to let them know they are on your mind. When we remain connected in truth and in love, we are able to challenge each other in ways that keep us from being self-deceived. Let's use the time we have to connect with others, for relationships are what matter most in this life.

❑ Act of Courage

Think of three people you can encourage today.
Send them a text, a gift, or have a chat with them.
Don't forget to be intentional in your encouragement!

Join God's Purposes

Jonah was greatly displeased and became furious. He prayed to the LORD, "Please, LORD, isn't this what I said while I was still in my own country? That's why I fled toward Tarshish in the first place. I knew that you are a gracious and compassionate God, slow to anger, abounding in faithful love, and one who relents from sending disaster."

JONAH 4:1-2 CSB

Jonah knew God to be merciful, slow to anger, and abounding in love. He knew if anyone repented, they would find favor and shelter in God's mercy. Interestingly, that is exactly why he fled from his assignment to go to Nineveh. Though God was ready to restore the people of Nineveh, Jonah did not feel as kindly toward them.

Are you holding a grudge against someone? Do you avoid praying for that person and refuse to connect with them? Perhaps you should take Jonah's lesson to heart. Even though you resist forgiving as Christ has called you to do, he will often give you the opportunity to do what is right.

☐ Act of Courage

Today you have the opportunity to join with God's heart and purposes. Will you, or will you find yourself deterred from running from your assignment?

Direct Communication

"Do not nurse hatred in your heart for any of your relatives. Confront people directly so you will not be held guilty for their sin."

LEVITICUS 19:17 NLT

Bitterness grows in the crevices of our hearts when we allow grudges and misunderstandings to keep us from connecting with others. Confronting people about how they hurt you can be scary and make you feel vulnerable. Instead of cutting people off without so much as a word, be willing to do the hard thing. Have an honest conversation.

You should be able to let go of anything that you are not willing to confront in another person. If you cannot forgive and move on giving them the benefit of the doubt, then you should have a conversation. It is much braver to face your fears and tell the truth instead of continuing with misplaced assumptions and wrongly held offenses.

☐ Act of Courage

Be honest with others about how their speech and actions affect you. It is not a virtue to pretend not to care and then allow bitterness to grow in your heart.

New Every Morning

The steadfast love of the LORD never ceases;
his mercies never come to an end;
they are new every morning;
great is your faithfulness.

LAMENTATIONS 3:22-23 ESV

Every new day is a fresh opportunity to experience the incredible mercy of God. As the sun rises our senses awaken, and we are faced with a brand-new morning. Today has never happened before. Even in the rhythms of the mundane there is something fresh and new happening. May we learn to awaken with eyes which search out God's goodness.

When we mindfully remember God is the author of this day and every day before and after today, we can rest in trust. He will not abandon us. He is with us. There is fresh faith for our hearts. He is moving in mercy. Even on the worst days of our lives, tomorrow dawns with a new perspective and a new opportunity.

☐ Act of Courage

Read today's verse and journal about it. Perhaps rewrite it in your own words. Start each day this week meditating on this verse and the reality and opportunity it holds.

Good Things

Fix your thoughts on what is true, and honorable, and right, and pure, and lovely, and admirable. Think about things that are excellent and worthy of praise.

PHILIPPIANS 4:8 NLT

What are your thoughts consumed with these days? Perhaps you are constantly thinking about the headlines and the bad reports that continue to come in. Maybe you are spending too much time online comparing your life to the highlight reels of others, or you can't stop worrying about how you will pay that bill or figure out the logistics of care for a loved one. Or maybe it's just tough fighting off an incessant and underlying anxiety.

We are called not to ignore the world and its problems and needs, but to rise above it. We can be completely rooted in reality and still choose to set our thoughts on good things. Don't know where to start? Think of the good that is in your life already and the mercy of God on display. Thank God for it and continue to dwell on these kinds of things.

❏ Act of Courage

Make a list of things you can think about when you feel overwhelmed. Consider the thoughts that pull you back to the goodness of God.

Force of Love

There is no power above us or beneath us—no power that could ever be found in the universe that can distance us from God's passionate love, which is lavished upon us through our Lord Jesus, the Anointed One!

ROMANS 8:39 TPT

Love is the most powerful force in the universe. Why should we not then be preoccupied with it? God is love. The very makeup of the Creator of the world is love. No power can distance us from the passionate love of God because there is nothing more powerful than the persistent presence of God.

When you feel overwhelmed, attacked, or belittled today, remember this: God's love surrounds you. When you feel ill-equipped, overlooked, or just plain tired, remember: God's love consumes you. The force of his love broke the chains of sin and death and freed us from every form of darkness. Our Lord Jesus lavishes his limitless love on us right now. Selah.

☐  Act of Courage

Whenever you feel unsure today, remember God's love is with you. It's the same love that inhabits the very being of God. Just keep going in the power of his love.

Open and Honest

Better is open rebuke than love that is concealed.
Faithful are the wounds of a friend,
but deceitful are the kisses of an enemy.

PROVERBS 27:5-6 NASB

Honesty is not just about telling the truth, but letting others speak it as well. Someone who never utters a dissenting opinion may be hiding their true colors. Flattery may win many people over, but it does not build deep connections or trust. May we embrace the honest and sometimes harsh words of our friends who seek to build us up in love. May we be wary of those who only ever compliment us.

Deceit is not uncommon, but it is devastating. No one likes to be lied to. No one wants to find out that someone they trusted has broken their confidence. It is much better to lead with honesty than to try to avoid hurting someone's feelings by being disingenuous. We are all just trying our very best, so let's give others the opportunity to show up in honesty.

☐ Act of Courage

Don't hide your opinion from others when they ask for it, and don't try to soothe someone's ego by lying to them.

Eager Joy

You turned my wailing into dancing; you removed my sackcloth and clothed me with joy, that my heart may sing your praises and not be silent. Lord my God, I will praise you forever.

PSALM 30:11-12 NIV

Whether you are currently in a season of grief or you are in a season of calm, may you know the hope of Christ that covers you today. There is joy coming. If you have already experienced the breakthrough of this kind of relief, remember it. Remember the comfort, the deep connection, and the illumination you found in God's presence.

If you are waiting for that breakthrough, know that it is coming. Your heart will sing his praises and not be silent, for your joy will be overflowing! Your praise will rise to your Redeemer and friend. He is with you now, in the depths of your grief, and he will never let you go. Your time of celebration is coming. It's coming!

□ Act of Courage

Give God your joy, even if you have to remember better times. Ask him to come in the palpable mercy of his presence, and to lift the burden of your grief!

Growing Grace

The law came to make sin worse. But when sin grew worse, God's grace increased. Sin once used death to rule us, but God gave people more of his grace so that grace could rule by making people right with him. And this brings life forever through Jesus Christ our Lord.

ROMANS 5:20-21 NCV

The grace of God is not static. It is ever increasing. The worse the world gets, the more grace God gives. The harder our trials, the more grace he infuses into our souls. The grace of God is made complete in Christ. There is no greater measure than what Christ did to bring us to the Father. He broke the barrier that separated his presence from his people, and now we are all able to fellowship with him!

Grace empowers us to persevere in hard times. It helps us to choose the right thing when the easier thing would be to compromise. Grace moves our hearts toward the giver of life. Grace is our teacher, our covering, and our support. May we dwell in it, and may we offer it freely, for freely it is given to us!

☐ *Act of Courage*

Offer grace to someone who is struggling. Let them off the hook and give them room to heal and grow.

Passionate Devotion

Encourage the believers to be passionately devoted to beautiful works of righteousness by meeting the urgent needs of others and not be unfruitful.

TITUS 3:14 TPT

Passionate devotion to righteousness as described in this verse is not ambiguous. It is not caught up in super-spiritual descriptions of heart posture. It is simple: it meets urgent needs of others, and it is fruitful. Fruitfulness can be measured. It can be accounted for, and there is no need for imagination to find it.

How passionately devoted are we to God and to his righteousness? According to this passage of Scripture, we can find the answer in how generous we are to be with our resources and how intentionally we should spend our lives. May we spend it on what truly matters, which are the things that will last. Let's sow into others, giving more than we have been accustomed to. Let's sow seeds of the Spirit's fruit through every area of our lives.

 ☐ *Act of Courage*

Identify one way you can grow in your pursuit of righteousness and plan to implement it today!

Mind of Christ

Adopt the same attitude
as that of Christ Jesus.

PHILIPPIANS 2:5 CSB

When you consider what Christ Jesus must have thought about, what comes to mind? How do you picture him using his imagination? We know this much: Jesus had a close relationship with the Father, spending time in prayer before him every day. We know what Jesus taught, how he acted, and the effects of his ministry. As the Son of God, his thoughts were not far from the words that came out of his mouth. Jesus was not duplicitous.

We are familiar with our own thoughts. Do they reflect the values of God's kingdom? First Corinthians 2:16 offers us this: "We have the mind of Christ." That is, we have the Holy Spirit who reveals to us the thoughts and purposes of Christ. The Spirit offers revelations of God's kingdom to us enlarging our understanding and broadening our perspectives to see from his own.

☐ *Act of Courage*

*Spend time in prayer and ask the Holy Spirit to reveal
more of God's kingdom to your understanding.
As he does, share this with others.*

Reflections of Love

"In that way, you will be acting as true children of your Father in heaven. For he gives his sunlight to both the evil and the good, and he sends rain on the just and the unjust alike."

MATTHEW 5:45 NLT

Jesus said, "You have heard the law that says, 'Love your neighbor' and hate your enemy. But I say, love your enemies! Pray for those who persecute you!" (Matthew 5:43-44). In this way, we act as true children of God. Loving those who love us is not where the law of love ends. It loves *everyone*, no matter who they are or how they treat us.

Does this seem impossible? By the grace of God nothing is impossible. We show we are true children of God by the way we love others and not only those who like us! How we treat those who despise us is much more telling of the limits, or lack thereof, of our love. May we choose the harder way, the way of Christ, that places love above all other things!

❑ *Act of Courage*

Extend love to those who don't like you even if perhaps the feeling is mutual. This is the way of Christ.

November

Be strong in the Lord
and in his mighty power.

EPHESIANS 6:10 NIV

Stones of Remembrance

> Those twelve stones which they took out of the Jordan, Joshua set up in Gilgal. Then he spoke to the children of Israel, saying: "When your children ask their fathers in time to come, saying, 'What are these stones?' then you shall let your children know, saying, 'Israel crossed over this Jordan on dry land.'"
>
> JOSHUA 4:20-22 NKJV

When God moves on our behalf in significant ways, we can be intentional about setting up our own "stones of remembrance" in our lives. We don't have to use actual stones but anything that specifically represents breakthrough for us. When people, including future generations, ask us about the significance, we can share it with them. This will not only encourage them, but it will also cause us to remember anew.

When we look with hindsight, we can often see things more clearly than we could at the time. Our emotions have time and space to settle. May we share the goodness of God as we saw it in those times, being intentional about putting reminders around us so we will not forget what he has done.

☐ *Act of Courage*

What is one of the most significant breakthroughs you've had in your walk with God? Create something that signifies that moment and display it somewhere.

Lifted by Wonder

Lift up your eyes on high,
And see who has created these things,
Who brings out their host by number;
He calls them all by name,
By the greatness of His might
And the strength of His power;
Not one is missing.

ISAIAH 40:26 NCV

The same God who calls each star by name also knows your name. You are even more dear to him. He doesn't overlook a single comet, and he will not miss you. Whatever you are facing, God knows. Your most secret thoughts and longings are known to him. He will never use them against you. He is ever so loving, and he can be trusted with your secrets.

When was the last time you felt the awe of creation? Maybe you stood beside the ocean and felt how very small you are compared to it. Maybe a flower peeking through a crack in pavement made you stop in wonder at the beauty which blossoms in unexpected places. Connecting with nature is a wonderful way to ground yourself in the reality of God's handiwork.

☐ *Act of Courage*

Take a walk in nature during the day, or stand beneath the stars at night, and let your senses take in what you see.

Ready to Share

*Philip ran up and heard him reading Isaiah the prophet,
and said, "Do you understand what you are reading?"
And he said, "Well, how could I, unless someone guides
me?" And he invited Philip to come up and sit with him.*

ACTS 8:30-31 NASB

When Philip overheard a passing stranger reading from
Isaiah, he was moved to ask him if he understood it. Was
this by chance? No. The Holy Spirit moved him to walk
alongside the chariot. This man he encountered was
described as being an Ethiopian eunuch in the court of
the queen of Ethiopia. Though he did not understand the
prophet Isaiah's words on his own, God sent Philip to him
to explain.

God always sends help to those who are searching for him.
He lights the way, opening up our hearts in understanding,
often through the wisdom and revelation of others. Are we
as ready as Philip to share the good news of the gospel of
Christ? May we be ready to share the wonderful mercy of
God, and may we follow the pull of the Spirit that leads us
into these situations.

☐ *Act of Courage*

*Ask the Holy Spirit to guide you today, and listen to his
leading, even if it seems silly! Trust him and try it out.*

Completely Overflowing

He is the complete fullness of deity living in human form. And our own completeness is now found in him. We are completely filled with God as Christ's fullness overflows within us. He is the Head of every kingdom and authority in the universe!

COLOSSIANS 2:9-10 TPT

If we have any questions about what God looks like in humanity, we have someone to look to—Jesus Christ! Not only do we have his recorded teachings and the example of his life, but we also have fellowship with him right here and right now through the Holy Spirit. What a marvelous mystery it is that God fills us to overflowing!

Everything will be subject to Jesus one day. Nothing will escape God's notice. He will set every wrong thing right and restore his children to himself. He will redeem what seems to us to be irredeemable. He will not stop until every promise is fulfilled and the whole world is full of his glory. In the meantime, we have the fullness of God with us, transforming us from the inside out.

☐ Act of Courage

Ask the Spirit of God to fill you to overflowing with his love, peace, joy, and hope. Set your eyes on the Promise Keeper, who won't forget to fulfill a single promise!

In Parched Places

The LORD will always lead you,
satisfy you in a parched land,
and strengthen your bones.
You will be like a watered garden
and like a spring whose water never runs dry.

ISAIAH 58:11 CSB

The springs of God's mercy are always fresh and flowing no matter how dry the landscape of our lives appears. Even in an arid desert, the fountain of God's grace flows freely in our direction meeting our needs and strengthening our souls and bodies. He does this for all who walk in his ways!

As we share what we have with others, God replenishes our lives. When we care for others, he offers us what we need to continue. May we not only look for ways that God's mercy meets us, but how we can share it with others. As Isaiah 58:8 says, when we share what we have with the hungry and open our homes to those who have none, "Then your light shall break forth like the dawn, and your healing shall spring up quickly." Even in dry, difficult places we will find refreshment in God!

❑ *Act of Courage*

*Give as an act of making room to receive
even greater measures from the Lord.*

The Little Things

"One who is faithful in a very little is also faithful in much, and one who is dishonest in a very little is also dishonest in much."

Luke 16:10 ESV

Have you ever thought that a little compromise doesn't matter? Unfortunately, this is not true. How we steward the little things indicates how we handle bigger matters. Let's be diligent then, to do the right thing even in ways others may not even notice. Let's be purposeful in integrity, caring for what we already have rather than wasting the little that is ours in search of bigger and better things.

We may be able to fool ourselves into thinking we will be trustworthy with much, if only we could have that much. But this is utter nonsense. We need to take care of our resources, stewarding them wisely, if we truly want to be successful in the values of the kingdom. If we are faithful with what we've got, then whatever we are entrusted with will only continue to grow! If we are not faithful with what we have, then we need to focus on those things instead of getting caught up in the what-ifs or the possibilities.

☐ *Act of Courage*

Take stock of the person you want to be.
What do you want your life to look like?
Now evaluate what it is you already are responsible for.

Giver of Good Gifts

"Which of you, if your son asks for bread, will give him a stone? Or if he asks for a fish, will give him a snake? If you, then, though you are evil, know how to give good gifts to your children, how much more will your Father in heaven give good gifts to those who ask him!"

MATTHEW 7:9-11 NIV

God is a good Father. We've heard this countless times. Even imperfect humans know how to provide appropriate sustenance for their children. When kids ask for food, it is because they are hungry. A good parent will do all they can to satisfy that need. Even apart from necessities, parents are moved to bring joy to their children.

God does this as well, but even more lavishly than we ever could. When we have needs and ask God to meet them, he does not tell us to fend for ourselves or play cruel tricks on us. He meets our needs, and often he goes above our needs to satisfy the desires of our hearts. Psalm 22:26 says this: "The poor will eat and be satisfied; those who seek the Lord will praise him." Let's thank him for what he's provided and what he will provide!

☐ Act of Courage

When you are asked to meet a need, whether it's for family, friend, or stranger, don't just meet it; give extra.

Divine Exchange

To all who mourn in Israel,
he will give a crown of beauty for ashes,
a joyous blessing instead of mourning,
festive praise instead of despair.
In their righteousness, they will be like great oaks
that the LORD has planted for his own glory.

ISAIAH 61:3 NLT

Come to the Lord and trade your sorrows for his joy. Give him the ashes of your disappointment, and he will give you the beauty of his redemption. Instead of despair, your heart will sing in praise. Even when it is only an act of faith, don't quit coming to the Lord! He is your sustenance and will be your satisfaction. He will fulfill you beyond your wildest dreams!

There is never a situation God can't turn around with his mercy. Even what seems completely lost can be found by him. Let's not give up on the power of his love even if we have to loosen the details of what that looks like as we walk through seasons of hardship. He is not finished weaving his mercy into our stories, and there is still more beauty, blessing, and praise to experience!

☐ Act of Courage

Write down all of your worries;
pray line by line offering each one to the Lord.

Cycle of Blessing

Does your life in Christ give you strength? Does his love comfort you? Do we share together in the spirit? Do you have mercy and kindness? If so, make me very happy by having the same thoughts, sharing the same love, and having one mind and purpose.

PHILIPPIANS 2:1-2 NCV

In our union with Christ, his strength, encouragement, and comfort is for us to share with others! Our breakthrough becomes the launching point for others' breakthroughs. If we have received comfort, let's offer comfort. If we have been strengthened, let's offer strength to others not because we have it all figured out, but because we have resources and experience to offer!

It can be difficult to comprehend the power of communal exchange and sharing with others in a highly individualistic society. Yet this was not the culture of the early church. They were communal cultures. May we humble ourselves and learn to depend on one another in appropriate ways. May we actively look for opportunities to spread what we have received in order to share the wealth of our relationships.

❏ *Act of Courage*

Spend time in the presence of God and receive freely from his love.

Wise Living

Teach us to number our days,
That we may gain a heart of wisdom.

PSALM 90:12 NKJV

There is a tremendous amount of wisdom in knowing our days are limited. It's important to value our time and relationships each and every day. To take anything for granted on any single day we have been given is not just a loss; it is also grievous. For most of us, this only truly hits home through brushing up against tragedy or experiencing loss.

How intentionally are you living in the day-to-day? Are you pushing through, waiting for a time when things will be less busy before you start prioritizing in your life? If you have been on autopilot, take this as your cue to be more intentional with your time. Figure out what it is you want most out of life, and don't be afraid to go after it!

☐ Act of Courage

What are the things you want others to remember about you when you are gone? What do YOU not want to miss out on? Incorporate these things into your schedule and pare down the things that don't matter as much.

Nothing Can Stop It

Rivers of pain and persecution will never extinguish this flame. Endless floods will be unable to quench this raging fire that burns within you. Everything will be consumed. It will stop at nothing as you yield everything to this furious fire until it won't even seem to you like a sacrifice anymore.

SONG OF SONGS 8:7 TPT

Nothing can stop God's passionate love. We are familiar with both Paul's and David's declarations of this amazing love. Solomon, in Song of Songs, also describes this passion. God's love is like an all-consuming fire that burns up everything in its path and brings life to all it encounters.

The oceans could not quench the fire of love that burns in God's heart. Oh, that we would also burn with love for him in the same way! God's love is not polite, nor is it standoffish. It is a raging fire that is moved to be near the objects of his affection. May we surrender ourselves to the passion of his heart!

☐ *Act of Courage*

Invite God's love to cover you, and when you feel resistance in yourself, ask God to reveal his kindness toward you.

Unashamed

I am not ashamed of the gospel, for it is the power of God for salvation to everyone who believes, to the Jew first and also to the Greek.

ROMANS 1:16 NASB

The liberating power of God is good news to be shared. What difference has the gospel of Christ made in your life? How has the love of God changed you? May you remember what you discovered at first: God is good, and his liberating love removes your shame! May you rediscover the wonders of his fellowship as you think through your life in him.

If you find yourself coming up short when thinking through your personal experience of God's power, don't be discouraged. His gospel is more than words and ideas. It is transformative and productive. How have you grown since you surrendered to Christ? Have those in your life seen a difference? Hebrews 4:12 says, "The word of God is living and active." As long as you are alive, the Spirit works in you.

☐ *Act of Courage*

Share your testimony with someone today, not holding back because of what they could think of you.

Holy Persistence

Ruth replied: "Don't plead with me to abandon you or to return and not follow you. For wherever you go, I will go, and wherever you live, I will live; your people will be my people, and your God will be my God. Where you die, I will die, and there I will be buried. May the LORD punish me, and do so severely, if anything but death separates you and me."

RUTH 1:16-17 CSB

Naomi was on her way back to her homeland, a place she hadn't lived in decades. Her daughters-in-law, both widowed, were traveling with her when Naomi encouraged them to go back to the homes of their youth. While one daughter-in-law did, Ruth refused. Naomi had become her family, and she did not want to separate from her. She vowed to serve Naomi's God, and to be Naomi's companion and caretaker.

Ruth's persistence was burning within her. She could not imagine a different way of life other than to spend it with her mother-in-law even if that meant uncertainty and poverty. As the story goes, Ruth finds favor in the fields of a kinsman-redeemer. In the end, she and Naomi both experienced the redemption of God in powerful ways.

☐ *Act of Courage*

Don't let the reasoning of others change your mind about the path God is calling you to follow.

Wisdom's Voice

Happy are those who listen to me, watching at my door
every day, waiting at my open doorway.
Those who find me find life, and the LORD will be
pleased with them.

PROVERBS 8:34-35 NCV

When we intentionally look for wisdom, listen to its
perspective, and put it into practice, we will benefit. Even
those who follow wisdom's ways without digging into the
whys reap the rewards. As Proverbs 17:28 says, "Even fools
seem to be wise if they keep quiet; if they don't speak, they
appear to understand."

If you find yourself wanting to go beyond obedience
into a real relationship with wisdom, understanding why
wisdom leads in certain ways, then you must become a
student! Students do not passively learn; it is an activity
with participation and posture. May you sit at wisdom's
doorway every day, ready for the lesson that is yours to
learn. Give time each morning or evening or whenever you
can carve out undistracted time in order to relate to Jesus,
to learn the ways of his personified wisdom, and to be
open to his teaching.

☐ Act of Courage

*Read through a chapter of Proverbs and write down the
wisdom that stands out to you. Keep going back to it
throughout your week.*

So Much Better

"What no eye has seen, nor ear heard,
nor the heart of man imagined,
what God has prepared for those who love him."

1 CORINTHIANS 2:9 ESV

God has prepared goodness that meets us in the mundane of the here and now. This goodness will be overwhelmingly better when his kingdom comes to earth and every promise he ever made is fulfilled. This is all a reflection of the mercy and kindness of his heart toward us. Blessings we cannot even imagine are what God has in store for those who love him.

May our hope be bolstered and our courage strengthened as we meditate on the wonderful nature of God! May we come face-to-face with experiences that deepen our understanding of his goodness. May we be overwhelmed by the kindness of his mercy as it shifts our perspectives and allows us to see the connections of his Spirit to this world that are already all around us. May our eyes be opened and our hearts awakened to the wonders of his careful attention. He is so much better than we can ever comprehend!

☐ *Act of Courage*

Keep your attention open to seeing the cues of God's kindness in action. Dare to dream bigger as you experience his intention and mercy.

Room for Grace

My dear children, I am writing this to you so that you will not sin. But if anyone does sin, we have an advocate who pleads our case before the Father. He is Jesus Christ, the one who is truly righteous.

1 JOHN 2:1 NLT

There is a difference between a standard of excellence and a stringent expectation of perfection. How will we know what the goal is if it remains obscure? We have no hope of growing into spiritual maturity if we do not know the foundation and principles that lead to it. Failure to meet these goals is not cause to throw away the pursuit. There is grace for our weaknesses and our messes.

Jesus, who is with the Father, pleads our case as our holy intercessor. He knows we will misunderstand and mess up, and he offered himself as the go-between because he can offer what we never could—perfect love and complete surrender. Our great advocate does not dismiss us when we sin. He gives us grace as we humbly submit ourselves to him. His love covers our sin, fear, and shame, and we are made new in his mercy.

☐ *Act of Courage*

When you miss the mark today, don't let shame sideline you. Offer your willingness to change and your humble heart to the Lord, and then move on.

Inward Renewal

We do not lose heart. Though outwardly we are wasting away, yet inwardly we are being renewed day by day.

2 CORINTHIANS 4:16 NIV

Our bodies wear out gradually as we age. We can't escape this process! We all feel the limitations of our humanity. Whether healthy or sick, there is one kind of renewal that is promised to all in the same abundant measure: the renewal of our spirits.

Paul went on in verse seventeen to say, "Our light and momentary troubles are achieving for us an eternal glory that far outweighs them all." What troubles feel overwhelming to you at this stage in your life? They are but short-lived in the light of eternity. The unseen realm is eternal as Paul says in verse eighteen. This is the realm in which we encounter God. From Spirit to spirit he refreshes and renews us on the inside, bolstering our hope and giving us fresh peace, joy, and love along the way. There is always more—infinitely more—in his presence!

❑ Act of Courage

Focus on the inner health of your heart, soul, and mind. Ask God to refresh and renew you from the inside out!

Steady Reminders

I will always remind you about these things, even though you know them and are established in the truth you now have. I think it is right, as long as I am in this bodily tent, to wake you up with a reminder.

2 PETER 1:12-13 CSB

In order to stay in alignment with the ways of Christ we need to be reminded of his truths. We cannot simply listen one day and then mindlessly fall back into the conditioned routines of our life. We need reminders of the wonderful mercy, grace, and peace of Christ that was offered through his sacrifice once and for all. His sacrifice was not only for his disciples and the early church but also for us today!

We can so easily forget the struggles of yesterday in the presence of joy. We can also overlook the celebrations of last year, month, or week, when presented with the tension of the unknowns in our present and our future. This is why it is so important to remember where we've come from, what we've walked through, and how God's mercy has kept us steady through it all.

❏ Act of Courage

If you keep a journal, read through an old one. Are you surprised by what you have forgotten? Write down a few truths you want to remember from Scripture, friends, or your own heart. Post them in places you will easily see them.

Grace to Forgive

> At first there was no one I could count on to faithfully stand with me—they all ran off and abandoned me—but don't hold this against them.
>
> 2 TIMOTHY 4:16 TPT

Even though Paul had to stand alone during some of his trials while many of the new believers abandoned him, he encouraged Timothy to not hold this against them. Imagine a friend was telling you of a time when they were counting on being backed up, and everyone around them left them to stand on their own. Would you be gracious to those who abandoned them, or would you be angry with them?

Just as we have to choose to forgive others who abandon us in a time of need, may we encourage those who love us to also extend grace. Paul experienced the empowering presence of the Lord strengthening him to continue in his ministry even though he did it alone. In time he had others come alongside him, and so will we. May we be patient in the meantime, and may we offer grace to those who choose not to stay.

❑ *Act of Courage*

Ask the Lord to make his presence powerfully known to you in the areas you feel alone and forgive those who chose to leave you.

Don't Hide

They heard the sound of the Lord God walking in the garden in the cool of the day, and the man and his wife hid themselves from the presence of the Lord God among the trees of the garden.

Genesis 3:8 esv

In the aftermath of their sin, Adam and Eve hid from their Maker. Though they walked with God, they still did not understand the power of his love. When they awoke to their nakedness and frailty, they lost the innocence with which God created them. Instead of trusting the relationship they had with the Creator, they chose to take things into their own hands by eating fruit from the only tree in the garden that was restricted to them.

In that moment Adam and Eve knew shame, and it caused them to hide. How has shame driven you to hide? Whatever your embarrassment is, no matter how awful it feels to you, God is full of loving-kindness toward you. Jesus came to rid us of our shame and to bring us back to the fullness of a relationship with the Father. He has already done this! Will you come out from your hiding place and allow God to speak his words of life over you today?

☐ Act of Courage

Share with God what you haven't dared to share with anyone else, and let his love wash over you and set you free.

Loving Promises

You keep your loving promise and lead the people you
have saved. With your strength you will guide them to
your holy place.

EXODUS 15:13 NCV

God himself leads us as we look to him. We have no need
for a substitute, for Jesus Christ has removed all that stood
between God's presence and us. There are no more veils,
walls, or mediators needed. God's presence is with his
people, and all who come to Jesus and surrender to his
ways are his people.

What more could we ask for? And yet, there is so much
more love, grace, peace, joy, and hope found in his Holy
Spirit. His life within us is more satisfying than riches can
buy. God will not stop leading us. Even when the earth
quakes, nations fall, and chaos ensues, God is faithful. He
keeps his loving promises—every one of them!—and leads
the people he has saved. May we take incredible hope,
comfort, and peace in the presence of our God who guides
us through the deserts, storms, and high places of our lives.

☐ *Act of Courage*

Surrender your fear to God and follow him.
Even when you feel afraid, look to his loyal love
that never leaves you or abandons you.

Courage to Change

Let us search out and examine our ways,
And turn back to the Lord.

LAMENTATIONS 3:40 NKJV

It is a foolish person who never reevaluates their approach to life. The person who never examines their motivations may overlook the reasons they do things simply because that is how they've always done them. Much of our behavior is conditioned, so let's have the courage to discover what's at the root of our perceptions and actions.

How have we wandered from love? How have we made excuses for the lack of mercy, justice, and peace in our world? Let's get clear on what Jesus actually revealed about life in God, and let's be brave enough to be willing to change our minds and behaviors based on what we find. The truth of God has not changed though our understanding of it is always limited. When we align ourselves in God's love, we will find there is more room for humility, grace, and transformative mercy.

☐ Act of Courage

Take a good look at your lifestyle habits and your attitudes toward others. What lines up with Christ's teachings and what doesn't? Be courageous enough to admit when you're off and turn back to the Lord!

Boundless Grace

In the ages to come He might show the boundless riches of His grace in kindness toward us in Christ Jesus.

EPHESIANS 2:7 NASB

When you think of God's grace what comes to mind? Do you ever consider the grace of God as a limited resource? We know through Christ that the grace of God is immeasurable. It is as abundant as his mercy! The riches of God's grace and kindness are infinite and limitless. May we never put restrictions on what God does not himself impede!

In this verse there is the implication that God's people will be the visible display of this boundless grace and kindness. When you consider the church and its reputation, do you think this is true? Though you cannot change the actions of others, you can certainly choose your own approach. Whatever restrictions you have put around God's grace, whether out of fear, ignorance, or your own insecurities, be courageous enough today to let God's grace be bigger than your experience or control. Good news: there is grace to empower you to do this!

☐ *Act of Courage*

Be willing to evaluate where you have put limits on God's grace either in your life or in the lives of others and ask God to help you let go of them.

Imperfect Conditions

Farmers who wait for perfect weather never plant.
If they watch every cloud, they never harvest.

ECCLESIASTES 11:4 NLT

This is such an important reminder; those who wait for the
perfect conditions to start their endeavor will never do it!
There will never be a perfect time to make a significant
change. Yet we can know the season we are in and act
accordingly. When it's planting season, we should plant.
We cannot expect the fruits of harvest to appear magically
in a field where seeds were not sown.

Is there something you know needs to happen, but you
have continued to put it off? Take this as your cue to move
ahead and do the work. Make an actionable plan, and then
do the mundane work necessary at the beginning that will
pave the way for the fruitfulness of the harvest season.
Throw away the excuses and just begin. You don't have
to know how it all will go. Just do the consistent work
necessary to affect the change you want to see.

☐ Act of Courage

What is it you want to build in your life?
Make a plan and then take the first step toward it.

Strength of Faith

"Have you believed because you have seen me? Blessed are those who have not seen and yet have believed."

JOHN 20:29 ESV

It takes courage to believe what we have never seen with our own eyes or touched with our own hands. Thomas, whom Jesus was speaking to in this verse, insisted that in order to believe that Jesus had been resurrected and had previously appeared to his disciples, would have to see the wounds of the nails that had crucified Jesus. He wanted to put his hand into Christ's sides where he had been pierced.

Jesus, being gracious, appeared to Thomas and told him to do just that. Then he told Thomas to not give into his doubts any longer but to just believe. "Blessed are those who have not seen and yet have believed." May your faith strengthen in Jesus Christ as you experience the liberating love of his sacrifice through the Holy Spirit. May you allow yourself to hold space for the mystery, and also to hold onto the palpable peace of his presence.

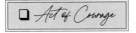

☐ Act of Courage

Read through Hebrews 11 to encourage you in your faith, and let your heart believe the goodness of God!

Not a Single Thing

> There is no power above us or beneath us—no power
> that could ever be found in the universe that can
> distance us from God's passionate love, which is lavished
> upon us through our Lord Jesus, the Anointed One!
>
> ROMANS 8:39 TPT

What causes you to question the love of God? Does sickness, war, or the poor choices of powerful leaders lead you away from grace? We can't ignore the questions that come up, but we can certainly allow the love of God to permeate our understanding of the circumstances around us. Even the most traumatic events in this life cannot separate us from the powerful love of God.

May we have the courage to look to Jesus when all else is falling apart. May we have the tenacity to hold on to him, to allow his love to hold us, and for his peace to fill us as we weather the storms of this life. There is *nothing*—no power, no nuclear weapon, no wicked leader—that can distance us from God's passionate love. What a wonderful truth to meditate upon today.

❑ *Act of Courage*

Write out everything that worries you , both in the world at large and in your own life and ask the Spirit to cover those things with his palpable, loving peace.

But First

"Seek first his kingdom and his righteousness,
and all these things will be given to you as well."

MATTHEW 6:33 NIV

Surely you've seen those shirts that say, "But first, coffee."
It is wise to build habits that set us up well for the rest of
our day. Drinking coffee is a pretty universal way to receive
energy to face the tasks ahead of us.

Whether you are a coffee drinker or not, do the things
you start your day with include seeking the kingdom
of Jesus? How do you make space for fellowship with
Christ within your schedule? Is it an afterthought or a
priority? Fellowship with Christ is a pleasure as is coffee
for many people. Make time, especially before jumping
into something big for the day, to spend time with Jesus.
Take a Jesus break in the afternoon. As you spend time
with him, the pleasure of doing so will only grow. The little
things add up, so don't overlook what even a few minutes
focusing on his presence can do for you!

☐ Act of Courage

*Be intentional about spending time in the presence of the
Lord today even if it is a few minutes here and there!*

Refuge and Deliverer

The LORD is my rock,
my fortress, and my deliverer,
my God, my rock where I seek refuge,
my shield and the horn of my salvation,
my stronghold.

PSALM 18:2 CSB

As real as the ground under your feet is the reality of the presence of God. He is the shield who surrounds you, your champion deliverer, and your mighty victory! Run into the shelter of his presence, and rest. There is grace to empower you, peace to calm your anxiety, and love to completely cover you.

God is both a place of refuge and a mighty deliverer. The same God who delivered David from his fears is the one who fights for you. The brilliance of his presence will break through the stormy nights that overcome your life. He is the safest place, the firmest foundation, and the most trustworthy ally you can imagine. Call out to him, and he will answer. Turn to him, and he will reach out and cover you. When you are afraid, run into the fortress of his love!

❑ *Act of Courage*

Do not belittle yourself for feeling fear. We all experience it, and God's expectation isn't for you to be immune to it. In your fear, turn to the Lord, and he will meet you.

Simple Requirements

He has told you, O man, what is good, and what does
the LORD require of you but to do justice, and to love
kindness, and to walk humbly with your God?

MICAH 6:8 ESV

This verse is a simple explanation of God's values. Why do
we complicate what God has simplified over and over again
in his Word? Jesus' teachings all lead back to the foundation
of God's requirements: love God, and love others. In the
book of Micah, doing justice, loving kindness, and walking
humbly with God are all expressions of this love.

May you have the courage to get rid of misconceptions
about doctrine and theology that complicate what God has
made simple. May you not put requirements upon yourself
or others that God does not put on us. What marvelous
mercy, what generous grace, what humble kindness he
shows us over and over again. May we endeavor to act
toward others as God acts toward us. He is good, faithful,
and true. He is kind, steadfast, and full of justice. Do good
to others, walk humbly with God, and love kindness. It is
that simple!

☐ *Act of Courage*

*Ask God to show you the simplicity and power of his love
and implement that same kindness in your expectations
and relationship with others.*

Hope Restores

> "May he also be to you one who restores life and sustains your old age; for your daughter-in-law, who loves you and is better to you than seven sons, has given birth to him."
>
> RUTH 4:15 NASB

After Ruth had married Boaz restoring the hope of a future line for Naomi's family, there was redemptive joy in Naomi's life and heart. Ruth and Boaz's son was a tangible sign to the woman that God had not forsaken her. The women around Naomi said, "Blessed is the Lord who has not left you without a redeemer today, and may his name become famous in Israel" (verse 14).

The little boy was named Obed, and he was the grandfather of King David. We know now in the hindsight of history that God not only brought redemption to the life of Ruth and Naomi, but it was in this very lineage that Jesus the Messiah was born! Naomi and Ruth had both been widowed and destitute. Even so, God turned their situation around and brought beauty out of the ashes of their devastation. He can do it for you too!

☐ *Act of Courage*

Identify what feels hopeless in your life and offer it to God. Ask for his redemptive love to give you hope for the beauty he will sow from the ashes of your disappointment.

December

Search for the LORD and for his strength;
Continually seek him.

1 CHRONICLES 16:11 NLT

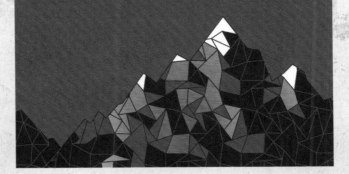

Patient Strength

We then who are strong ought to bear with the scruples of the weak, and not to please ourselves.

ROMANS 15:1 NKJV

Maturity in the Lord leads to patience with others. Those who have learned to embrace others in their naiveté, giving grace to where they are at, are filled with the humble love of God. This comes through time, perspective, and often, experiencing the gracious patience of others toward us. There is a reason that patience is a fruit of the Spirit! It allows us to lean into the relationships we have and see the gifts of present grace for what they are.

Whether you identify with this type of spiritual maturity or not, may you allow for the mistakes of others all while continuing to press on in love. Don't let the impatience of others rush you to side with something that will not stand the test of time. Give your time, your attention, and your energy to the things that last. The things that produce faith, hope, and love will outlast and overcome weaknesses both in your life and in the lives of others.

☐ Act of Courage

Practice patience in your interactions with others today, not rushing to share your opinion, but letting them learn through experience.

It's Coming

"Never again will they hunger; never again will they thirst. The sun will not beat down on them,' nor any scorching heat."

REVELATION 7:16 NIV

The book of Revelation describes what is coming, the hope we can currently have, and the warnings about the end of the age. Though many go without essentials now, there will come a day when no one will hunger or thirst anymore. All of their longings and needs will be met in the fulfillment of Christ's glorious kingdom on earth. They will not suffer under heat exhaustion or wonder where they will get their next meal.

Even now as we await that day in hope, may we practice the generosity of meeting the needs of those who have less than us. It is a faith practice to do this! Don't we want to represent our Father well on this earth? When we care for widows and orphans, when we feed the poor and offer restorative solutions for those who have been devastated by disaster, we reflect the power of God's love moving through us. May we look ahead with hope, and may we also pursue peace in the present time.

☐ Act of Courage

Feed someone today as an act of generosity and goodwill.
Be a reprieve, a gulp of refreshing water,
to those who struggle.

Don't Overlook Sacrifice

Looking at him, Jesus loved him and said to him, "You lack one thing: Go, sell all you have and give to the poor, and you will have treasure in heaven. Then come, follow me."

MARK 10:21 CSB

When you've heard or read this passage of Scripture before, what is the key thought you took away? Did you feel disconnected from the wealth of this man and therefore distancing yourself from identifying with him? Or did you simply overlook it because the call Jesus made to him did not appeal to your own desires? Wealth is a tool. Money is not the root of all evil; the love of money is. This rich man had a huge decision to make. Did he love Jesus or love his wealth more?

We could ask ourselves the same question. Do we value our comfort more than the call of Christ? Do we love the ease that wealth brings, only caring for our own needs and building ourselves little castles that cut us off from others? Do we trust our own choices more than we trust the wisdom of Christ? Sacrifice is required for following Jesus though it will not look the same for each of us. Between you and God, what is it he is asking you to do?

☐ *Act of Courage*

Ask Jesus, who loves you, what you can do to follow him without restraint.

Fear Cannot Conquer

Lord, even when your path takes me through
the valley of deepest darkness,
fear will never conquer me, for you already have!
You remain close to me
and lead me through it all the way.
Your authority is my strength and my peace.
The comfort of your love takes away my fear.
I'll never be lonely, for you are near.

PSALM 23:4 TPT

Fear cannot conquer those who are completely covered in the love of Christ. This is not to say we will never experience fear, but that fear cannot completely overwhelm or disarm us, for the perfection of God's love is even more overwhelming.

In Psalm 56, David said, "In the day that I'm afraid, I lay all my fears before you and trust in you with all my heart." Let's put our total trust in God who remains close to us and leads us all the way through the valleys of deepest darkness. No matter how heavy it feels God is with us. He is our authority and peace. The comfort of his love takes away our fear. What a gloriously good God!

☐ Act of Courage

When fears rise within you lay them all before God and trust him with your whole heart. Remember he is near, and he will never leave you.

Woven Together

An enemy might defeat one person, but two people together can defend themselves; a rope that is woven of three strings is hard to break.

ECCLESIASTES 4:12 NCV

With God all things are possible. With the encouragement and support of a friend we are able to fend off an attack. With both the support of another and the help of God, there is a strength that is hard to break.

Do you have a friend, family member, or significant other who is trustworthy? Do you stick together no matter troubles come? Rooted in the help and strength of God's love, you can go even further together than you could on your own. May you not neglect the meaningful relationships in your life; rather, may you hold close the ones which are trustworthy, loving, and supportive. Friends and family give strength! No need to go it alone in life, for we were created for relationship.

 Act of Courage

Prioritize your relationships with trusted friends and family. Instead of isolating yourself lean into the safe relationships in your life and be sure to let them know when you need their help.

Called by Name

O Jacob, listen to the LORD who created you.
O Israel, the one who formed you says,
"Do not be afraid, for I have ransomed you.
I have called you by name; you are mine."

ISAIAH 43:1 NLT

When you are afraid, may you hear the Lord's voice saying over you as he did to Jacob, "Do not be afraid, for I have ransomed you. I have called you by name; you are mine." He has done it! This is not wishful thinking. Your Maker pursues you with passionate love. He covers you with his powerful mercy. He has redeemed you through the blood of Jesus.

John 3:16-17 says: "This is how God loved the world: He gave his one and only Son, so that everyone who believes in him will not perish but have eternal life. God sent his Son into the world not to judge the world, but to save the world through him." God's redemption does not judge you; it saves you. Believe in Christ, answer the one who calls your name, and come home to his love.

☐ *Act of Courage*

When you feel anxiety rising, close your eyes, take a deep breath, and remember God calls you by name. He has redeemed you. You are his. Breathe it in until you feel grounded and full of peace.

Still in Process

By one offering He has perfected forever
those who are being sanctified.

HEBREWS 10:14 NKJV

How is it possible that, in Christ, we are at once perfectly
holy and yet still being made holy? We are all in process
in this world. Not one of us has reached the goal. Take
Paul's statement in Philippians 3, when he said he had not
yet reached the goal of absolute fullness. Still, he kept
pursuing it.

Christ's sacrifice is sufficient. Nothing can be added to it or
taken away from its power. It is all we need to be made right
with God. That is all! In this sense we are already perfected
in Christ. At the same time, we know that in our humanity,
none of us is perfect! We will still make mistakes. It is in this
process we are refined, remaining humble before the Lord
and others, and continually transforming to Christ's image as
we follow him. We are being transfigured into his image as
we go from glory to glory (2 Corinthians 3:18)!

□ Act of Courage

*Let no shame keep you from pursuing the Lord, and also
recognize there is grace for your mistakes as you live your
life. Have courage to allow for both realities to be held in
tension and find your freedom in Christ's love.*

Freedom

The Lord is the Spirit, and where the Spirit of the Lord
is, there is freedom.

2 CORINTHIANS 3:17 NIV

Where is the Spirit of God? Where does he dwell? David
pushed this point by asking these questions in Psalm 139:
"Where can I go from your Spirit? Where can I flee from
your presence? If I go up to the heavens, you are there;
if I make my bed in the depths, you are there" (139:7-8).
He goes on, but the conclusion he comes to is that there
is nowhere he can run from God's presence. Not even
darkness can hide us from his view.

This same Spirit that is everywhere is the one who offers
us complete and total freedom! We are transformed by
the glory of God, having nothing that separates us from
the love of Christ. Where the Spirit of the Lord is, there
is freedom. There is liberation in his love. Wherever you
are today, there the presence of God meets you and
completely covers you. Let him set you free from whatever
holds you back today, for being stuck certainly isn't what
he wants for you!

☐ *Act of Courage*

*Invite God into the areas where you feel stuck, lonely,
and afraid. He is already near, and where he is there
is freedom for you!*

Live without Intimidation

Don't be intimidated by those who are older than you; simply be the example they need to see by being faithful and true in all that you do. Speak the truth and live a life of purity and authentic love as you remain strong in your faith.

1 TIMOTHY 4:12 TPT

Are you intimidated by those who are older, seem to be more put together, or who have more education than you? God does not work in intimidation tactics, nor does he promote them in any of his followers. There is a difference, certainly, between feeling intimidated because of our own insecurities, or being actively coerced by people who hold power over us.

Don't let your insecurities keep you from doing what is yours to do. Stop comparing yourself to others and follow the leading of the Lord in your life. No two people tread the same path. This life is yours, and you get to live how you choose to. Don't give away your autonomy. Only you can decide what you will do, put up with, or pursue. Focus on what you can do to honor the Lord and others. This is your responsibility; what other people think is not!

❏ *Act of Courage*

Don't let the fear of others' perceptions keep you from pursuing what is on your heart.

Delightful Obedience

Samuel said: "Does the LORD take pleasure in burnt
offerings and sacrifices
as much as in obeying the LORD?
Look: to obey is better than sacrifice,
to pay attention is better than the fat of rams. For
rebellion is like the sin of divination, and defiance is like
wickedness and idolatry. Because you have rejected the
word of the LORD, he has rejected you as king."

1 SAMUEL 15:22-23 CSB

If we put on a good show of how "holy" we are, we are no
better than the religious elite whom Jesus rebuked. What
truly matters is how we live out the love of God with mercy,
justice, kindness, and peace. Obedience to the Lord is as
important as sacrifice. What kind of relationship do we have
if we have it out of popular expectation but reject listening
to the One who asked for the sacrifice to begin with?

Take time to listen to God's voice today. Perhaps you
already have an idea of what he wants you to do but
you've been dragging your feet and waiting for a different
option to show up. It is because God loves you that he
directs you. Do you trust his heart? Do you trust his
intentions? He is better than anyone you know. He does
not manipulate, trick, or deceive. He is faithful, merciful,
and kind.

❑ Act of Courage

Offer God your obedience instead of bargaining with him.

Thoughts of God

He is the one who makes the mountains and creates the wind and makes his thoughts known to people. He changes the dawn into darkness and walks over the mountains of the earth. His name is the Lord God All-Powerful.

AMOS 4:13 NCV

God is not just the powerful Creator, he is the God who shares his thoughts with us. He set the earth in motion, put the stars in the sky, spoke the mountains and rivers into existence, and made every creature on land and in the sea. He is everywhere, and he cannot be contained. This God is the one whom Jesus called Father and who pursues us with passionate affection through his Spirit.

Do you know the sweet fellowship of the Holy Spirit? Have you ever had a realization that seemed to come from outside of yourself but made things come together in a way that was both seamless and profound? Perhaps it was God sharing that specific thought with you. Revelation and wisdom come from him, and he does not hide his goodness from those who seek him.

☐ Act of Courage

Ask God to reveal a deeper understanding of his thoughts, his ways, and his purposes to you today. Ask him to share his thoughts with you!

Kindness that Leads

Do you presume on the riches of his kindness and forbearance and patience, not knowing that God's kindness is meant to lead you to repentance?

ROMANS 2:4 ESV

The kindness of God leads us to repentance. Second Peter 3:9 says that God is patient with us—how kind!—so we have the opportunity to repent. May we not take God's extraordinary kindness for granted. His tolerance and patience do not mean he condones our actions. If we are not aligned with the law of Christ's love, humbly surrendering to his ways, and living out his mercy toward others, we still have the chance to repent.

Repentance is not simply saying, "I'm sorry." It involves turning away from our sin and turning toward God. It means changing the way we act toward others if we have not been caring enough already. It requires a reformation of how we do things. If you would be kinder to those who are kind to you, how much more should you transform under the kindness of God!

☐ Act of Courage

Be honest with yourself about whether there is anything in God's love you are using as an excuse to sin. If there is, be courageous enough to make a change.

The Same God

This same God who takes care of me will supply all your needs from his glorious riches, which have been given to us in Christ Jesus.

PHILIPPIANS 4:19 NLT

Paul encouraged the Philippians to take hope from his own experiences with Christ. The same God who took care of him will also supply all our needs. Even when the odds are stacked against us and we are going through hard times, God will supply his overwhelmingly sufficient grace to meet our needs.

There is also another principle at work within this verse. Paul had just acknowledged and expressed gratitude for the gift the Philippians had sent to him. In following it up with this verse, that the same God who takes care of him will also take care of them, Paul is illustrating the divine blessing of generosity. The more we give, the more room we have to receive from God. Even if it seems small in our eyes, it may be just the thing to bring breakthrough and encouragement to another. Let's be generous, therefore, trusting God will also provide for us, especially when we share what we have with others!

❑ Act of Courage

Give a portion of what you have with someone who has less than you today, and trust God to meet your needs!

He Remains

I know that everything God does will remain forever; there is nothing to add to it and there is nothing to take from it. And God has so worked, that people will fear Him.

ECCLESIASTES 3:14 NASB

Nothing can be added to or taken away from the work God does. This is good news especially in the light of Christ. All that Jesus came to fulfill has already been fulfilled. His sacrifice opened the door for us to know and worship the Father in Spirit and in truth with nothing separating us, not the thick veil of the temple or the thinnest gauze over our eyes. God provided all we need to experience the freedom of his love. He broke down every barrier and removed every hurdle.

There is now no condemnation for those in Christ! Romans 8:2 continues to explain that the law of the Spirit of life flowing through Jesus has liberated us from the law of sin and death. We are free from the consequences of sin and death all because of what Jesus did! When all else fades away, Jesus remains. The Father remains. The Spirit remains. His love remains. Praise the Lord!

☐ Act of Courage

Give God all your stresses and worries today and keep bringing your attention back to his lasting love.

None Other

From long ago no one has ever heard of a God like you.
No one has ever seen a God besides you.
You help the people who trust you.

ISAIAH 64:4 ESV

The God of the Bible is a God who helps his people. Not only this, but through Christ we see that God is a loving Father and a faithful friend. He is an advocate for the vulnerable, and he is a promoter of the humble. He lifts up those who have no strength to stand on their own. He helps everyone who calls on him no matter their language, age, class, or status.

Who else is so magnanimous in mercy? Who shows no favoritism to the rich and powerful, but instead honors those the world deems lowly? He is better than we can imagine, but let's stretch our imaginations, nonetheless! How different this world would be if everyone who claimed to love Christ sought to be like this. Let's follow the example of our God, laying down our pride and partnering with his compassion, mercy, and justice.

☐ Act of Courage

*When someone asks for your help today, don't put it off.
Do it right away, if possible.*

Banner of Love

"In that day there shall be a Root of Jesse, Who shall stand as a banner to the people; For the Gentiles shall seek Him, And His resting place shall be glorious."

ISAIAH 11:10 NKJV

The royal family line of Jesse was prophesied through Isaiah to be the line from which the Messiah would come. We know that Jesus, the son of Mary, was the fulfillment of this promise. He stood as a banner not only to the people of Israel but to all who believed in him as their Savior. He is the ruler of the nations!

Jesus Christ is the furthest thing from exclusionary. There are not only a few who are saved through faith in him; all who come to him are welcome! May we love with this same kind of welcome. May we be hospitable to strangers and immigrants, treating everyone with the same dignity Christ offers us. No one is less worthy than another, so let's lay down our biases and love with open hearts!

☐ Act of Courage

Are there any fear-based or prejudiced biases you can recognize in your thinking? When they come up, lay them down before Jesus and choose to live in the kindness of his love that serves as a banner for all!

Light of Truth

The Light of Truth was about to come into the world
and shine upon everyone. He entered into the very
world he created, yet the world was unaware.

JOHN 1:9-10 TPT

When you turn on a light in a dark room, what was once hidden from sight is now illuminated. Jesus came to the darkness of humanity shining his light of love on everyone. He revealed the liberating love of the Father that was never meant to stay under wraps or misunderstood!

John 1:5 says, "This Living Expression is the Light that bursts through gloom – the Light that darkness could not diminish!" Jesus is the Light of Truth that darkness could not diminish. Though he was crucified, though many ridiculed his ministry, the flame of his love could not be extinguished. The grave could not hold him, and neither can anything else. He is the victorious one, the crowning champion over death. He is our liberator and our Redeemer! What a joy it is to know him, to serve him, and to love him.

❑ *Act of Courage*

*What feels too overbearing for you is an opportunity to
lean into the power of God's love that broke every burden
of sin. Invite the light of Jesus to shine on your mind
and to shift your perspective.*

The Mystery

Just as you cannot understand the path of the wind or the mystery of a tiny baby growing in its mother's womb, so you cannot understand the activity of God, who does all things.

ECCLESIASTES 11:5 NLT

There is mystery that ties all of our understanding to the unknowable. Though science has breakthroughs that explain many of the discoveries in nature and humanity, there is still more being discovered all the time! Though we know the hows of babies growing and the certain patterns of nature, we still do not know the deeper whys, but God does.

Instead of demanding answers for everything before we venture to trust, let's allow for the mystery to move us in wonder. We should not abandon the realities of this world, but we should also not let those realities hinder our faith in God. They can go hand-in-hand. God's ways are higher than our ways, and his thoughts more intricate than our own. May we trust his nature, knowing our own understanding will grow with time.

☐ *Act of Courage*

Lay down your pride and be willing to admit what you do not know or are not sure of.

Preparer

> "It is he who will go as a forerunner before Him in the spirit and power of Elijah, to turn the hearts of fathers back to their children, and the disobedient to the attitude of the righteous, to make ready a people prepared for the Lord."
>
> LUKE 1:17 NASB

John the Baptist prepared the way for Jesus' ministry. He stirred up hearts and pointed them toward the coming Christ. Matthew 3:2 states the message of John's ministry as this: "Repent, for the kingdom of heaven is at hand." Turning back to God and away from sin, this was John's admonition to those who listened.

Why was John necessary? Perhaps much like a farmer breaking up the soil and tilling it, he prepared the hearts of people by breaking up the fallow ground. When Jesus came their hearts were ready to receive the seeds of his ministry and teaching. God is purposeful, and he knows what he is doing. May we recognize the important parts we all play in his kingdom, though they may look different for each of us.

☐ Act of Courage

Give up trying to meet the status quo and live with integrity and authenticity. It takes courage, but it's so worth it!

The Favor of God

> He came to her and said, "Greetings, O favored one, the Lord is with you!" But she was greatly troubled at the saying, and tried to discern what sort of greeting this might be. And the angel said to her, "Do not be afraid, Mary, for you have found favor with God."
>
> LUKE 1:28-30 ESV

Mary was a teenager when the angel appeared to her telling her she would become pregnant with a son. She was engaged but not yet married. This favor that God bestowed on her would not look like favor to anyone else and perhaps not even to her. God chose Mary to carry the Messiah, to be his mother. What an honor! But all of this had yet to play out. What could she truly know of what the angel told her?

Have you ever felt ill equipped for something you were tasked to do? Perhaps it was given as an honor, and yet you could not feel the honor in it. The favor of God does not always look like favor. It does not mean wealth, comfort, or ease. And yet it is the highest form of honor to be trusted by God! May we see the blessing where others miss it, leaning into the love and grace of God.

☐ *Act of Courage*

Trust that when God offers you a gift, it is good even when it feels like a burden at first.

Abiding Joy

"I have told you this so that my joy may be in you,
and that your joy may be complete."

JOHN 15:11 NIV

Jesus had just told his disciples they needed to abide
in him, the true vine. When the branches are connected
to the source, they can bear much fruit. But if they are
disconnected from the vine, all life dries up. Why did Jesus
tell them these things? He said in verse eleven, "so that my
joy may be in you, and that your joy may be complete."

When we yield to Jesus, dwelling in his love, we are directly
connected to the source of all life. Our lives will bear the
fruit of his kingdom and his Spirit as it flows from his
presence and power in and through us. What a beautiful
testimony this is! What joy is ours when we lean on the
love of the Lord. What powerful reciprocity there is in this
union!

☐ *Act of Courage*

*Instead of trying to figure out how to be your best self on
your own, learn to love others the way Christ loves you.
Rely on his powerful presence in your life,
and the fruit of his life in you will be evident.*

Mindful of the Word

> Keep this Book of the Law always on your lips;
> meditate on it day and night, so that you may
> be careful to do everything written in it.
> Then you will be prosperous and successful.
>
> JOSHUA 1:8 NIV

What we fill ourselves with, that is the fruit which will spill out of our lives. What we spend our time on, what we watch, listen to, and read, all affect not only our mindsets but also our expectations.

What can you recite from memory? What songs are always in your head and on your lips? May you be mindful of what you repeat. Maybe the songs you used to love you now notice don't represent your values at all. Maybe it's not how you want to think, speak, or approach life. You can take control over your thoughts by being intentional about what you let into your mind. This is not limited to media, but also to conversations, teachings, and doctrines.

☐ *Act of Courage*

Identify and write down your core values. As you become more aware of your thoughts, recognize what is out of alignment with these words. Find a verse, a phrase, or a song lyric to redirect you and bring you consciously back to your values. Repeat it in those necessary moments.

True Children

> When the fullness of the time had come, God sent forth His Son, born of a woman, born under the law, to redeem those who were under the law, that we might receive the adoption as sons.
>
> GALATIANS 4:4-5 NKJV

We are children of God, welcomed into his family through Jesus Christ. Each of us who belong to him are not strangers, weird neighbors, or distant relatives. We don't live as slaves to the law but as dearly loved sons and daughters. We are heirs of God through Jesus, the Messiah.

This is almost too much to take in and comprehend. The creator of all things—the maker of heaven and earth—is our Father. Let's not go backwards into the bondage of religious expectation. Rather, let's press into the relationship we have with God through Christ. What child does not delight in spending time with their loving parent? May we find ourselves drawn to him in every trial, every question, every celebration, and every joy. Let's come boldly to him, for we have access through his Son!

☐ Act of Courage

Let every prayer you pray and good thing you do today be an act of love toward your Father who delights in you!

A Son Is Given

A child is born to us, a son is given to us. The
government will rest on his shoulders. And he will be
called: Wonderful Counselor, Mighty God, Everlasting
Father, Prince of Peace.

ISAIAH 9:6 NLT

The Son of God came as a humble baby. He depended on
his mother to feed him and his father to house him. He
did not come out of the womb proclaiming the day of the
Lord. He had to learn what all children have to learn: to
communicate, to walk, and to become independent. Even
though Jesus was the Son of God, we must remember he
was also a man.

How readily do you identify with Jesus' humanity? It
can be hard to imagine him through the lens of history
knowing what we know. He was tired, hungry, and maybe
even irritable at times. He was tempted. His voice might
have cracked as he entered puberty. He experienced loss.
Whatever makes you feel so alone in your struggles, Jesus
is familiar with. Take it to him as a friend and ask him to
reveal his heart to you.

☐ Act of Courage

*Remembering that Jesus was human as much as he is God
will open the door for you to trust him with your secrets.*

Glorious Grace

The Word became a human and lived among us. We saw his glory—the glory that belongs to the only Son of the Father—and he was full of grace and truth.

JOHN 1:14 NCV

The grace of God became flesh when Jesus was born. Those around him grew to know his character, his quirks, and his habits. In the Bible we have record of the many miracles he performed and the way he bucked tradition in order to share the love of God with those who wouldn't spend time at the Temple. He came to show everyone the way to the Father, and that is what he actually did.

Jesus was full of grace and truth, spreading the wonderful news of God's mercy with all who would listen. He moved in miraculous love to heal, provide food, calm storms, and raise the dead. He did this so we would truly know he is the Son of God. Let's take his glory seriously. It is a wonder to behold!

☐ *Act of Courage*

Give God the glory he is due today and offer Jesus the deepest parts of your heart. Let his truth pierce your mind and allow you to surrender to his love.

Tangible Power

The entire crowd eagerly tried to come near Jesus so they could touch him and be healed, because a tangible supernatural power emanated from him, healing all who came close to him.

LUKE 6:19 TPT

Imagine being in this crowd of people knowing if you could just get close enough to touch Jesus you would be healed. Sickness is not an indictment on our character, and it is certainly not a punishment from God. It can cause people to go to extreme lengths doing whatever it takes to experience relief.

Jesus was like a walking, talking, healing fountain. People flocked to him so they could experience a bit of his power for their own breakthroughs. Jesus did not simply heal them though. He taught them as well. He taught them what matters most. He taught them what the kingdom of God is truly like. He revealed the mysteries of God to these common, desperate people. So, too, he reveals his truth to us in our own desperation. He meets us with the healing of his presence. He calms our fears. He brings peace, joy, and hope. He is so wonderful to us!

☐ *Act of Courage*

Let your needs drive you even closer to Jesus.

Good News

> The mighty Spirit of Lord Yahweh is wrapped around me because Yahweh has anointed me, as a messenger to preach good news to the poor. He sent me to heal the wounds of the brokenhearted, to tell captives, "You are free," and to tell prisoners, "Be free from your darkness."
>
> ISAIAH 61:1 TPT

The exceedingly good news of Christ is not for an elect few but for all. Jesus is the anointed King who reigns over all. He heals the wounds of the brokenhearted. He sets the captives free. He opens blind eyes. This is how wonderful he is, and yet we can never comprehend just how thoroughly glorious his love actually is.

When was the last time you heard really good news, the kind of news that made your heart swell and your mouth shout with joy? Picture it, and let your mind take you to that place. What did you feel, what did you see, and what did you hear? Tune into that moment and let it overtake you. When you come out of it, carry that joy with you into the rest of your day and let it fuel your wonder, peace, and expectations.

☐ Act of Courage

Tell someone about the best news you've ever heard, and how it impacted your life.

Living Hope

Blessed be the God and Father of our Lord Jesus Christ.
Because of his great mercy he has given us new birth
into a living hope through the resurrection of Jesus
Christ from the dead.

1 PETER 1:3 CSB

Jesus' resurrection from the grave was not just his victory;
it is also ours. We have a living hope; one that speaks
about all that is to come, all that has already been fulfilled,
and everything being sustained in the present moment.
May we have eyes to see what is coming and not let our
senses grow dull in the monotony of the mundane.

We cannot, nor should we, try to escape responsibilities
in our lives. How we live in the day-to-day matters greatly.
It is with time that rocks are worn down by water, cutting
a path through instead of going around. If we will be
persistent in our hope, applying the ways of Christ in our
homes, jobs, and communities, we will experience the
breakthrough of his power over time!

☐  Act of Courage

Be willing to keep persevering in hope in the little things.
Follow-through matters!

Completely New

If anyone belongs to Christ, there is a new creation.
The old things have gone; everything is made new!

2 CORINTHIANS 5:17 NCV

Our past loses its power over us when we submit our lives to the love of Christ. Being enfolded into his love, we are completely made new. We are not simply patched or renovated; we are fresh and new. Jesus compared it to being born again as a fresh new babe, innocent of the world and its ways. It's a fresh new start for us all.

May we have the courage to live out the changes God has made within our hearts as we abandon the selfish pursuits of our past. Any destructive behaviors that kept us from the full freedom of God's love should be avoided at all cost. There is so much grace, but let's take the momentum of a new start to be intentional about the changes we make!

❑ Act of Courage

Decide which things do not serve your life in Christ well. Think about those choices that don't promote love, truth, and justice, and make a change. Be sure to include what you will replace your poor choices with, taking time to consider what it is you want your life to radiate.

Learn to Wait

Those who wait for the LORD
Will gain new strength;
They will mount up with wings like eagles,
They will run and not get tired,
They will walk and not become weary.

ISAIAH 40:31 NASB

In these liminal days between Christmas and New Year's Eve, don't rush to move ahead too quickly. Today can be a day of rest and renewal. It can be a day in which you lean into the waiting. In good times, waiting teaches us how to anticipate. In hard times, it teaches us how to persevere.

Whatever frame of mind you find yourself in, whatever emotional state you are in, may you find that the grace of the Lord is near. Those who wait for the Lord will get divine strength. When you are weak, God offers you his own strength. You do not have to do anything more to prove yourself or suck it up. Lean in. Lean into the empowering grace of God. Here, you will find the strength to soar like an eagle.

☐ Act of Courage

Rest in the presence of God and let yourself off the hook with your to-do list. Wait on the Lord, and rest in his arms. Then you will have the strength you need to press on tomorrow.

What Awaits You

Though you started with little,
you will end with much.

JOB 8:7 NLT

We can sometimes read Scripture and romanticize its meaning to the original hearer. Job had just lost his whole family. Reading through the whole story, we know this was not a punishment from God. But his friends didn't know this. They went on little information and made assumptions they were ill-equipped to make. Still, they encouraged him to pray to God and seek the favor of the Almighty.

Job lived with integrity, and he did not deserve the tragedy of losing his family and his home. Still his integrity led him to wrestle through his grief and even question God yet persist in worshiping him along the way. In the end his friend's prophetic statement proved true, "Though you started with little, you will end with much." God is a Redeemer and a restorer. Press on in hope even if you feel as if you are beginning again. He always has more in store for those who love him!

❑  *Act of Courage*

Lay out your disappointment before God and trust he will redeem what you cannot change. He is so good, and he is not finished writing your story yet!